# A Discovery of Cinema

## THOROLD DICKINSON

LONDON · OXFORD UNIVERSITY PRESS · NEW YORK · TORONTO · 1971

*Oxford University Press, Ely House, London W. 1*

GLASGOW NEW YORK TORONTO MELBOURNE WELLINGTON
CAPE TOWN SALISBURY IBADAN NAIROBI DAR ES SALAAM LUSAKA ADDIS ABABA
BOMBAY CALCUTTA MADRAS KARACHI LAHORE DACCA
KUALA LUMPUR SINGAPORE HONG KONG TOKYO

Clothbound edition SBN 19 211439 5
Paperbound edition SBN 19 211440 9

© Oxford University Press 1971

Printed in Great Britain
by Fletcher & Son Ltd, Norwich

# Foreword

To the frustrations of the population explosion which occurred with the growth of industry in the nineteenth century the film offered a panacea. Theatre and music-hall were unable to meet the need for distraction and, as cinema expanded, these old forms of entertainment were thrust aside by the brash newcomer. One result has been a rise in quality in the theatre, which despite all pessimism has attracted new audiences. This law of survival has repeated itself in North America and Great Britain with the explosion of television. Cinema has been forced to shed much of its fat as theatre had to do a generation before; or, it would also be true to say, weeding out has allowed potent ideas which were being strangled to be aired.

For those who care, there is an urgent need to be aware of the growth in the structure of cinema, its erratic development, the physical and metaphysical influences which bear down on it. No film is an island: each is a variant link in a chain; each cannot but reflect—however frivolous or unrealistic the subject— the human condition at the time of its making. The present is only a moment linking past and future—the roots, the growth to date, the possibilities for further growth—and to this future the student can make one contribution, that of being ready for it.

There are some who can still remember the early stages of film-making, but among the young who take the film for granted the present state of the process is all important. Numbers of zealots are eager to practise the craft. But practice is governed by the technology and materials available at the time, and with the rapid discarding of old and adoption of new processes the time for thought battles against the time needed to digest and enjoy the flood of technological change. This short monograph on the evolution of cinema is an attempt to link film-maker and student, to relate achievement to the means available. It is not a history of the cinema, it is a personal view of a medium of expression which already in the short span of seventy-five years has often revealed itself as an art.

It is not in the scope of this work to survey animation film. This avoidance is prompted by admiration, not by indifference. The subject has been adequately covered by some remarkable books, based on first-hand knowledge, listed in the Bibliography. In this vast subject there have already been works which employ both forms; and in factual films the diagram and model have always had a place alongside live action.

The material of this volume derives from my own experience and study, which from 1925 onwards has been concerned with the human cinema only.

*Slade Film Department*
*The Slade School of Fine Art*
*University College London*

*March 1970*

# Contents

# List of Illustrations

Film Stills

*Note: Although the aspect ratio of films has changed in recent years, that of the still photographs issued for the purposes of publicity ('publicity stills') has been kept in the traditional ratio of 10″ × 8″, presumably to avoid the expense of altering the dimensions of the show cases at the entrance to cinemas. By this means also the same still cameras can be used as before.*

# Portraits

# Acknowledgements

This short study derives from a cycle of three lectures given to the English Federation of Film Societies in 1967, at Queen's College, Belfast in 1968, and at the American Film Institute's first Teachers' Seminar at the University of California in Santa Barbara in the same year.

My thanks to Lynton Lamb for proposing the book, to Professor George A. Huaco for permission to quote from and refer to *The Sociology of Film Art* (Basic Books Inc., New York, 1965), to my colleagues Mrs. Liz-Anne Bawden and Ian Tregarthen Jenkin for encouragement and support, to Mrs. Helen Coppin, Miss Susan Lermon, and Roger Davies for wisdom at the right moment, to Lutz Becker for research on the illustrations, to Robert Morgan for the diagrams and for technical advice, to Miss Julia Huntley and Miss Marian Binney for secretarial help, and to my wife Joanna for helping to sift and reshape a mass of notes into the form of a book and for the indexing. She joins me in dedicating this work to the wives of all film-makers.

For permission to reproduce photographs acknowledgements are due to: Sovfilm export, Moscow, for Eisenstein's work drawing; La Cinémathèque française for stills of F. W. Murnau directing *The Last Laugh*, Jean Renoir with Claude Renoir, and Marcel Carné directing *Les Visiteurs du soir*; Pressens Bild, Stockholm, for the photograph of Bo Wideberg in New York; Connoisseur Films Ltd., London, for the still from *La Grande Illusion*; Contemporary Films Ltd., for that from *La Règle du jeu*; Miss Marie Seton for the photograph of Satyajit Ray; M-G-M for that of Greta Garbo with Ramon Navarro; to the National Film Archive for all other stills; and Arthur Witmann of the *St. Louis Post Dispatch* for the photograph on the title page.

# The Tools and the Illusion

The moving image is a craft using twentieth-century technology, which, when human imagination transmutes sight and sound into something new, becomes an art. Other media have existed for thousands of years, the projection of the moving image for seventy-five, and for those of us who have grown up with and love this medium the novel sense of latent magic that is inspired by the sight of a blank screen is never lost. How can a two-dimensional image provoke emotional release and stimulate the intelligence? The power to change people, to induce good deeds and bad deeds, even to unhinge minds temporarily, to give us truth and beauty, is distilled before our eyes. And the prosaic dimensions of this screen act dynamically on the images thrown on to it.

Moving images are conceived to match the needs and the adequacies of the screens on which they are intended to be shown. The toy screen in the home belittles everything other than the home-movie. The astute television craftsman avoids the spectacular image, which is appropriate only to the giant curved screen, curved to hold the whole width of the screen equidistant from the source of the image, the lens in the projector. For the artist it is not merely a matter of size, it is a question of scale.

Illusion begins physically. As Ivor Montagu[1] describes with wit the mechanical and chemical processes involved in film-making, here I will only insist that in fact for 30% of the time during which a film is apparently on the screen, the screen is blank. A rain of 16 or more frames or images hits the screen every second during the projection of a silent film, and 24 frames per second during a sound film, and one third of the blanks occur while the image is being changed. The appearance of continuity is not achieved by the persistence of images on the retina of the eye but because of the slowness of the brain to sort out the impulses transmitted from the retina.[2] The appearance of continuity is maintained mentally in accord with the creative ability of the film-maker, like a conjuror, to keep the ball of illusion airborne.

The moving image is a one-eyed medium. On the two-dimensional screen there is an absolute need to create an illusion of a third dimension to encourage suspension of disbelief. On film it is done most directly by moving the camera.

[1] In *Film World* (London, 1963), pp. 1–92.

[2] In the opening sequence of *Men of Two Worlds* (1945) in the performance of a piano concerto during a wartime lunch-hour concert at the National Gallery in London, the beginning of the final passage of the music is matched with a long shot of the orchestra taken from directly overhead. It is a plan of the orchestra and for a split second this unfamiliar picture does not register. To make the shot appear to begin simultaneously with the music, which was already familiar, we found we had to start the picture two frames—which is one-twelfth of a second—ahead of the sound since it took the brain that amount of extra time to compute the unfamiliar sight.

You can test this on a train journey through the outskirts of a town where streets of terraced buildings lie at right-angles to the railway tracks. As you watch these blocks of buildings pass, look first with both eyes; then close one eye and you will get much the same effect with one eye as with two so long as the train is in motion. In monocular vision without movement, all is flat; with movement there is the illusion of a third dimension.

Back in 1913 the Italian Giovanni Pastrone made a landmark with his film *Cabiria* by, among other innovations, moving his camera laterally and slightly above the level of his foreground. Ten years later in 1923 Carl Mayer, scripting *The Last Laugh* for F. W. Murnau, proposed the forward movement of the camera at appropriately dramatic moments as if to thrust the spectator into the action of the film, and they found that this too could work unobtrusively. Hitherto it had been considered so obtrusive as to be suited only to a travel film.

The silent film was much closer to ballet and music-hall than to literature or theatre. But in the early days of silence the evolution of its indigenous capacity to originate illusion was severely manacled by the influence of the theatre; and as we will see later on this was to occur again in the period of the arrival of sound. These first explorers had nothing to which they could refer; everything that happened posed a new question to which they had to invent an answer. It took the pioneers ten years of trial and error to achieve some semblance of form, and while stumbling towards the solutions which would prove to be the foundations of cinema they were earning their bread and butter.

The process has continued and will continue indefinitely. The addition of sound and colour have carried the medium to astonishing levels of technological sophistication beyond the dreams of the pragmatic pioneers. As products of technology neither sound nor picture are realistic. Colour remains as synthetic as black and white has always been; but both can now be controlled in an immense range of variations. It is now possible even in colour to hold in sharp focus every object in view, as Lumière did in black and white when the train stopped by his camera in 1895. According to the choice of lens, distances can appear more or less remote, mountains more or less menacing. Focus can be softened until the object seen sharply becomes framed in abstractions—blobs of significant colour. Tempo is first under control in the camera within the shot, and later from shot to shot in the cutting-room during editing. Montage (the juxtaposition of picture against picture during editing for aesthetic or intellectual reasons) can be used with no concessions to fragmentation, to utility. These possibilities belong to sound as much as to picture, perhaps even to a greater extent, since modern microphones and recording equipment allow for the subtlest differentiation in tone, pitch, and perspective. The quality of the recording, the orchestration, and the sound-mixing of speech effects and music profoundly affect the impact of the picture. These new technical achievements have freed the sound film from the bonds of the written document and the drawing-board and have aided improvisation. The conventional studio is out-of-date other than for use where artificial settings are required. The more sophisticated production equipment of today can be packed on trucks and used on the site of the film. Life can be caught unrehearsed, unplanned, such material later blended with scripted work under controlled conditions.

The beacon, the culminant feat of all this complex, is that the imagination shall fuse the myriad elements into the mysterious compound which has been summed up by Robert Bresson: a film is not something photographed, it is something on its own.

In practice the range of film entertainment is wide. It tends to divide into two streams, and film study in America makes the distinction as between the *movie* and the *film*. The *movie* is for popular entertainment.[1] It is the product of an industry dominated by the producer in which there is no individual film-maker but a team or unit under the producer's control. The producer hires one or more writers who complete the bulk of their work before the director is engaged to work from their script. On this the rubber stamp *final* is more than a formality: the script is not to be tampered with. The director's work is done when the shooting is finished or as a concession when the first rough editing is done. The producer and editor are responsible for the final version and the director has no means of redress if he finds his intention distorted in the outcome. With their habitual precision, the French describe this kind of director (who is an interpreter like an orchestral conductor) as a *metteur-en-scène*, a term borrowed from the theatre.

The movie is the journalism of cinema where success is measured by the quantitative response of the public. It was the mainstay of cinema during its first sixty years, particularly in the U.S.A., Britain, and Asia. Money is a vital tool in film-making and the successful movie has financed the technical innovations from which all cinema has benefited. But it only survived by lapping up the new ideas for which every showman has to look if he is not to be left behind. These new ideas were and are being tested by the pioneers and nonconformists, the film-makers (in French, *réalisateurs*), whose work adorns the

---

[1] This convenient differentiation is also commercial. In Britain the number of 35 mm. copies of a *movie* in circulation usually exceeds forty, while the demand by art houses for a *film* is met with five copies at most, dwindling in time to one only or even none at all. See the note on Antonioni's *L'Eclisse* on page 151.

3

higher reaches of cinema and is described as *film*, the personal statement of an author who is his own producer and director.

The *movie* is explicit and complete in itself. Its audience is passive. The *film* is not complete: it poses implications which stimulate the audience. It involves the audience. In India the *movie* is virtually the only form of entertainment of any kind available: there is a minimal and uneconomic audience for the *film* which can only be made for export.

*Film* (the entertainment offered to the more sophisticated) and *movie* (shown at the big, popular cinemas) vary from country to country. Some of the elements have nothing to do with aesthetics. The film in a foreign language or dialect is harder to appreciate; even if it is a British *movie*, it will be regarded by most Americans as a *film* if some of its words and all its accents are alien.[1]

The popular audience hates to split its visual interest between the moving picture and the sub-titled translations of foreign dialogue[2] and prefers a spoken translation recorded later by a different team of actors, a process known as dubbing.[3] To the minority this is sacrilege, though they unwittingly accept it in nearly every film from Italy, where it is customary for actors to speak in their own language and for Italian speech to be dubbed over their lip movements after the film has been edited. To see and hear a performance from the same actor is rare in an Italian picture.[4]

Some subjects qualify for both kinds of audience. In Asia *The Seven Samurai* (1954) was as popular as any Western. Most of its points are made visually and the action is picturesque and stimulating. In Europe and North America it was shown with sub-titles to minority audiences with such success that it was remade in the U.S.A. with familiar actors against a Mexican background (nearer home in setting and physiognomy) and became popular as *The Magnificent Seven* (1960). Comparing the two films makes an interesting study.

[1] When in English there is a choice between a word of Latin derivation and one of Anglo-Saxon, the Americans prefer the former (e.g., elevator), the British prefer the latter (e.g., lift). The accent differential, too, is a real barrier in the U.S.A. It begins in New York where they say of a British film: 'Well, I got most of it', to the mid-west and beyond where they just adore your accent and then ask: 'But what exactly are you saying?'

[2] A new French process of sub-titling prints the lettering in the blank space which occurs between each frame of the picture except in anamorphic (i.e. CinemaScope) prints. But conservatism among film exhibitors inhibits them from changing the shape of the screen to accommodate the new position of the titling.

[3] As a film-editor I used dubbing as early as 1932. In the first case, to remove an inadequate sub-plot from a completed film, I dubbed new dialogue, spoken by the leading lady, over some of her close-ups in order to bridge the gaps in the story. When audiences failed to notice this, I improved an inadequate performance in another film by synchronizing the actress's best visual performance with the speech from shots in which she had spoken her lines better. Some reviewers singled out this synthesis as one of the best performances in the film.

[4] See 'Italy Sotto Voce', *Sight and Sound*, vol. 37, no. 3, p. 146.

Aesthetically, a simple touchstone is the test of predictability. If you can settle into a film without seeing it from the beginning, the reason is that this has been calculated: you are not required to grapple with any point at all. This is the commercial intention of the *movie*.[1] The story must flow effortlessly, no point must be explored too deeply. Characters must be few and small parts must be types rather than individuals. An audience which expects more than this from their entertainment demands as Diaghilev did of the young Jean Cocteau: 'Astonish me'. In the ideal commercial situation the entertainment carries on its surface all the predictability that lulls the mass audience while beneath the surface lie more stimulating nuances. In the early days Griffith achieved this in the idiom of his time, until the First World War shook the public out of their cloak of Victorian sentimentality and left him with the garment as a shroud. Chaplin throughout his career, the longest in cinema, has only missed this target in his later years.

The *film* which makes demands without compromise is an acquired taste, difficult for those accustomed to stimulation by the word rather than the picture. Such a film is normally the personal statement of an artist, a film-maker, a *réalisateur*. If he is not the original author, but like Shakespeare he transmutes the ideas of another and makes them his own, he deserves to be named the author. It is wholly unjust, however, invariably to give the main credit to the director of a film of which he has merely done the staging. Film reviewers who find this convenient have no right to call themselves critics. One should learn to differentiate between reviewers and critics as one should between *metteurs-en-scène* and *réalisateurs*.

## The Changing Process of Cinema

In the seventy-five years of cinema's duration, nearly all who have made a name in films have been self-taught. In the early days they were naturally self-guided too. There persists, therefore, a mistrust in the teaching of cinema since the more successful have been too busy to teach and have only given guidance out of self-interest. When later in their careers they have found time to stand back from the practice of cinema and take stock, they tend to believe only in the achievements of their heyday and mistrust, because they do not understand, the innovations which have come later.

From these seventy-five years it is possible to pick out perhaps seventy-five names which have influenced cinema. The majority are film-makers, then

[1] Outside American movie houses until recently it was the custom not to advertise the programme times and to stress the idea of continuous performance.

come script-writers, designers, and the smallest number of all are critics and theoreticians. Very few have had a lasting influence: some in trying to move forward have been forced off course, have landed up in a dead-end. For instance, under the influence of the theatre during the late 1930s, we were convinced by the films of Marcel Carné, *Le jour se lève*, *Quai des brumes*. Thirty years later they carry little conviction, seem theatrical, artificial period pieces, in the context of today.

There is now an increasing subtlety in the handling of human character and its conflicts in relation to its environs. If these are contemporary, communication between film-maker and audience is reciprocal. The frame of reference for both is our time. A rare faculty is needed to be able to resurrect the past credibly, or make imaginary worlds live.

In his book *The Sociology of Film Art*,[1] George H. Huaco examines three 'schools' of film-making that were complete in themselves and the reasons for their rise and fall. They were German (silent) Expressionism following defeat in the First World War, Soviet (silent) Expressive Realism following the Bolshevik Revolution and preceding the first Five-Year Plan of 1929, and Italian (sound) Neo-realism following the collapse of Italian Fascism.

He concludes:

Within each historical setting we have explored the impact of political, social, and economic variables on the exigencies of film production and on the rise and fall of the particular wave of stylistically unified film art. We have shown that each wave began only when four necessary structural forces were already present: (1) a cadre of trained film technicians, directors, cameramen, editors and actors; (2) a basic film plant including studios, laboratories, raw stock and equipment; (3) a mode of organization of the film industry which was either favourable or tolerant toward the ideology of the future film wave; (4) a climate of political norms which was either favourable or tolerant toward both the ideology and the style of the future film wave. We have seen how each film wave lasted only as long as these factors were present and how the gradual elimination of one or more of these factors was accompanied by the gradual decadence and eventual destruction of the particular film wave.

As an insider, I would vary and extend his theory. For me, the four structural factors are:

(1) Current events and achievements. These produce the 'climate of political norms' which Professor Huaco places fourth. Yet each of the three waves which he discusses was undoubtedly triggered by the whole political climate of the time: it could not have happened otherwise.

[1] New York and London, 1965.

(2) The creativity of film-makers (rather than Mr. Huaco's cadre of trained film technicians). It is the individual artist who influences his team of craftsmen, if they are well chosen, to co-operate, to carry out his ideas in all their novelty just as professionally as they have executed the more conventional ideas to which they have been accustomed.[1]

(3) The development of the mechanical and chemical and electrical means to exploit new ideas (rather than 'a basic film plant'). The equipment has to change, becoming more flexible to cope with new ideas.

(4) The capacity of a sufficient audience to appreciate the results. Time and again an interesting innovation has come to a dead-end because the film proved too costly for the market capable of assimilating it. It is normal to discount distribution and exploitation as a commerce and yet a film is only alive when it is being screened to an audience, and the diffusion of cinema is a science which requires as much study as production. I substitute this proposition for Mr. Huaco's third point: his favourable mode of organization of the film industry, which overlaps mine but does not stress enough the importance of the public.

Perhaps the two approaches may be broadly characterized as the American (*movies* made by teams) and the European (*films* created by individuals). Yet already in America the trend in the 1960s is towards independence for the film-maker and the transfer of mass-production from cinema to television.

The successful advance of cinema depends on the neck-and-neck alignment of these four elements or rather the capacity of the last three to keep up with social and political trends. Certainly none of the three waves mentioned earlier would have risen without the thrust of world war and revolution to hurl them forward. Writers on film aesthetics who do not take these matters into account are wilfully working with blinkers narrowing their field of view.

It is interesting to note that each of the three schools discussed by Professor Huaco grew up during a time of national emergency and around an abundant source of subject-matter which scattered ideas in all directions. In the case of the Soviet school it was the urgent need to change the climate of opinion from capitalist to socialist. In the German and Italian schools, as Professor Huaco infers, it was the presence of two prolific writers, Carl Mayer, an Austrian steeped as an art critic in the pursuit of expressionism, and Cesare Zavattini, a socialist who began life as a journalist and dramatic critic. Neither of them ever made a film on his own. It should also be noted that the

---

[1] Compare the conventional romantic style of the Mexican cameraman, Gabriel Figueroa, with the stark, realistic style which Luis Buñuel persuaded him to adopt in *Los Olvidados* (1950) and subsequent films.

7

finest hour of British cinema was during the Second World War when an enlightened group of enthusiasts in the temporary Ministry of Information harnessed the resources of the film industry to further the war effort, ranging in output from public entertainment of an escapist or patriotic nature to private instruction on every conceivable topic. In addition the War Office alone had 300 training films in production at one time. In the nominally international medium of cinema, the peaks of achievement are almost invariably national in inspiration: it is by their clarity and universality of expression that they become international.

The first phase of cinema was the period of the silent monochromatic and later orthochromatic film which lasted for some thirty years from the end of 1895 when regular public exhibition first began with the Lumière Brothers' programmes in the basement Indian Room of the Grand Café, Paris, until 1927 when the American public heard Al Jolson speak a monologue in *The Jazz Singer*. It was in 1927 also that panchromatic film was generally introduced in Hollywood, eventually displacing orthochromatic film.

Phase Two, the period of the early sound film, occupied another thirty years during which the dying influence of the silent film struggled with the theatre for possession of what was in fact an entirely new medium. The effect was a step backwards followed by a groping forward in a number of directions until mentally a new realism and physically the widening of the screen and restoration of the deep focus which had been a major element in orthochromatic film ushered in the third phase towards the end of the 1950s.

In this third phase the widening mental horizons of the time, the maturing of the first generation to accept cinema as part of life, and the fantastic leap forward in the invention and production of the tools of the trade have rocketed the possibilities of the medium.

The leading participants in these three phases were all non-conformists who refused to accept conventions deriving from existing forms of entertainment: the conformists' attitude to cinema is that if you can't beat it, join it and mould it in the ways to which you are already accustomed. This attitude may bring immediate profit from passive audiences, but in the long run stagnation and boredom drive even the passive, mass audience away from the cinemas. The abiding problem is to reconcile the conformist needs of commerce with the assets which only the non-conformists can provide.

New technical processes were introduced as a means to survival. The growing boredom of audiences during the 1920s challenged the four Warner Brothers to gamble on introducing the sound film at the risk of the heavy financial investment needed to install sound recording in studios and sound reproduction in theatres.[1] This decision put the industry deeply in debt to the banks which have been dominant ever since.[2] Later it was the loss of audiences to television that drove Twentieth Century-Fox to introduce the anamorphic lens[3]—again a heavy investment—which widened the screen, made depth of focus a necessity and so brought environment back into the picture.

[1] Warner Brothers began by recording sound on disc, but it was soon found that synchronization of sound and visuals was maintained better wth the sound-track printed optically at the edge of the picture, and sound on film quickly superseded the earlier, more cumbersome method.

[2] While European banks often choose to invest in separate film companies, studios, and productions, American banks prefer to lend money to producers at a fixed rate of interest, leaving all the gamble to their clients. Hence Hollywood's policy of producing for a quick return rather than being content to recoup their investment over a term of years. Hollywood can afford the *movie*, but it cannot afford the *film* except on the rarest occasions as a prestige gesture.

[3] 'Anamorphoser is the coined name to describe a cylindrical lens system which compresses a picture horizontally as it is taken and expands it in the same direction in projection. . . . The anamorphoser increases depth of focus. . . .' — H. Sidney Newcomer, M.D., in *New Screen Techniques*, see Bibliography.

# Aspect Ratio

35mm. full screen aperture (silent)
aspect ratio 1·33 : 1 approx.
0·980 × 0·723 in. picture

35mm. original sound aperture
aspect ratio approx. 1·2 : 1
probably 0·868 × 0·723 in. picture
centre-line of picture shifted to right

35mm. academy aperture
aspect ratio 1·33 : 1
0·868 × 0·631 in. picture

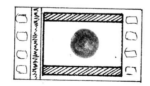

35mm. masked for widescreen
aspect ratio 1·85 : 1
0·868 × 0·447 in. picture
(sometimes shot as academy aperture
and masked to 1·85 : 1 in projection)

35mm. anamorphic (cinemascope, panavision)
squeezed image, squeezed 2 : 1 (width of
objects is half normal width)
0·868 × 0·735 in. aperture

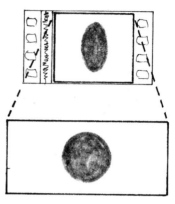

Projected appearance of 35 mm. anamorphic
image unsqueezed 2 : 1
dimensions of diagram relative to other
diagrams: 1·736 × 0·735 in.
aspect ratio 2.35 : 1

70mm. non-anamorphic with stereophonic
magnetic tracks (left, right, centre, control or
back-of-cinema) aspect ratio 2·2 : 1
1·913 × 0·868 in. picture
5 perforations high. No squeeze

16mm. silent film.
Perforation falls on frame-
line. 1 perforation per
frame, both sides of film
aspect ratio 1·37 : 1 approx.
0·402 × 0·292 in. picture

16mm. sound film. No
perforations on right
edge. Sound track in
their place. All other
dimensions same as for
16mm. silent film

# THE THREE PHASES OF CINEMA

**August Lumière**
1862–1954
**Louis Lumière**
1864–1948
Inventors

**Georges Méliès**
1861–1938
The Conjuror: acting and
directing in his *A la Conquête
du Pôle*

# Phase One
# The Silent Film

Many pioneers are conditioned, not born, and conditions can be as much negative as positive. The man who tries a new line out of dissatisfaction with his previous work has nothing to lose, is impelled from the past, not inspired by his prospects. There were many of these in the early days of cinema.

At first the negative film they used was monochromatic, sensitive to violet and blue and increasingly insensitive through green and yellow to red which failed to register even in its lighter tones. Experiment with additional dye sensitizers led to the introduction around 1918 of orthochromatic film, sensitive to green as well as to blue. The warmer colours, yellow through orange to red, still registered decreasingly and red continued to appear virtually black on the screen.[1] As the Caucasian is more of a red man than a white man, heavy creamy yellow make-up had to be used which drew embarrassing attention in public and caused chaos in street scenes. The natural colours of real surroundings were often rendered hideous, and black and white photography came to be known affectionately as soot and white-wash. The result was a strong inducement towards working in artificial settings inside studios with glass roof and walls.

But the great asset of monochromatic and orthochromatic film was its capacity for deep focus. In that earliest of Lumière's films *A Train Entering the Gare de Ciotat* (1895), a man's shoulder passing within a yard of the lens is as sharply in focus as the distance euphemistically labelled infinity. Even indoors this depth could be attained by using strong daylight or the artificial illumination of mercury vapour and arc light. The noise made by arc lighting was no drawback until the introduction of sound recording.

When thirty years later (1926) panchromatic negative film, sensitive to all colours including reds, began to be sold at an economic price in its first crude state, its weakest point was precisely the violet tone emphasized by arc lighting, which went out of fashion in favour of incandescent (yellow) light. But these lamps had not the penetration that arcs could attain, and 'stopping down' the diaphragm in the camera to achieve depth of focus reduced the amount of light reaching the negative to a point where scarcely any recognizable image could be registered. Therefore the diaphragm had to be kept more open: focus was shallow and a face in close-up was isolated from its environment which was blurred and therefore lost its importance, its insistent presence. The word began to take over the function of the visual, since sound was coming in at the time. The era of the canned play had begun.

Many people rock with laughter at the absurdity of primitive film. But does anyone imagine that artists and craftsmen of instant experience were

---

[1] There are no blacks in cinema since celluloid and emulsion are transparent, and this fact is oddly emphasized by the curious habit of framing the screen with a black border.

13

brought into the world by a robot God to understand this new invention without delay? Even the many inventors of cinema had no faith that it would outlive its novelty: they certainly had no clue to its potentialities.

At first the cinema was a recording machine, a kind of visual gramophone set up out of doors to record an event, or in a studio mounted on a fixed capstan before a stage on which was marked a white line. So long as the actor remained behind the line, he could be filmed from head to foot. To move the camera or cross the line was to invite dismissal. The public paid to see the whole actor as in the theatre. But what if a card game was involved? A close-up was made to identify the cards. Consecutive action was crowded on to one roll of negative. When the roll ran out, the scene had to be changed to avoid an unavoidable jump in the action at the beginning of the new roll.

Yet in the Paris Exhibition of 1900 there were colour films tinted by hand, talking films with Coquelin declaiming scenes from *Cyrano de Bergerac*, his voice roughly synchronized on a cylindrical phonograph record, there was a screen 53 feet high and 70 feet wide for spectacular scenes, and a Cinéorama with eleven projectors showing a complete circle of image which had been photographed from a balloon. The audience stood on the roof of the drum which housed the projectors: it seemed as if they were standing in the basket of a giant balloon whose underside bellied above them.

Where did these experiments lead? Eventually to the development of colour photography since hand-tinting was tedious and inaccurate, to the recording of sound on film since cylinder and disc lost synchronization when the film broke. In the exhibition a gale tore down the big screen, and the eleven projectors generated so much heat that the fire regulations were broken. But they were a brave try.

The cinema was developing in two directions, the theatrical picture and the living picture, which Siegfried Kracauer has described as the Méliès School and the Lumière School (Méliès the conjuror and Lumière the open-air photographer). A long tussle has been going on between them ever since, though in fact cinema aims at a judicious blend of both, so far as entertainment is concerned.

There are two aspects of the effect of theatre on film. Cinema as a two-dimensional silent record of a stage performance proved a hopeless investment once the novelty wore off. After a few years impresarios sought to raise the price of seats from pennies to shillings by filming Sarah Bernhardt, Eleanora Duse, Herbert Beerbohm Tree and the like in roles created by them in the theatre. In France the movement was called *le film d'art* to isolate it from the vulgarity of naturalism, still with no success. The theatre at

**Asta Nielsen**
1883–
in *The Joyless Street* (1925). The
first authentic screen tragedienne

second-hand and even at a tenth of the price has rarely been popular and even more rarely been justified.

On the other hand cinema has been consistently nourished by artists who got their training in the theatre and then abandoned the stage in favour of the film. Seven outstanding innovators, Max Linder, D. W. Griffith, Charles Chaplin, S. M. Eisenstein, Victor Sjöstrom, G. W. Pabst, F. W. Murnau, all grew up in the theatre but renounced it on finding greater satisfaction in the silent film.

We can now recognize the event that sealed the establishment of cinema as an accomplished fact. In the days when the entertainment served as a flash-in-the-pan, a novelty for the travelling showman, copies of films were sold outright and used by their itinerant exhibitors until they fell to pieces. Establishment came with respectability: shops, public rooms, and small halls were turned into cinemas and frequent changes of programme became necessary. Distribution of copies among the increasing number of exhibitors occupying fixed premises proved to be more economical than outright purchase of copies, even when the distributors demanded not a flat rate but a percentage of the cinemas' takings. The system began to take root around 1905 and it greatly increased the demands and the funds for production.

For the next ten years before the First World War the Latin cinema was dominant. The Italians introduced the long spectacular film *Quo Vadis?* in 1912, *Cabiria* in 1913. Their realistic dramas, like *Sperduti nel buio* (1914), were equally successful and earned stars like Francesca Bertini salaries which were not surpassed in Hollywood until after the First World War.

The introduction of Fascism in 1922 throttled this effort by political 'precensorship' which substituted bourgeois romantic escapism for realism, the boudoir for the bedroom, the chauffeur-driven car for the bicycle, the white telephone for the black. And the movement lay dormant until Luchino Visconti revived it with the blessing of Jean Renoir in his superb *Ossessione* in 1942, anticipating the collapse of the decadent régime in 1943. The term *neo-realism* coined by Umberto Barbaro acknowledged the resurgence of a school of realism which had amply justified itself thirty years before.

Surpassing the Italians in quantity of product, before the war of 1914, the French firm of Pathé alone used to distribute twice as much film in the U.S.A. as the whole American industry. It was Pathé who introduced the serial 'cliff-hanger' film to America, synchronizing release of the weekly episode with its syndicated publication in the local press. The French conjuror, Georges Méliès, founded his Star Film Company to distribute his own productions throughout America. The success of the comedian Max Linder's

*above*
**Max Linder** 1883–1925
The prototype screen comedian
*right*
**Charles Chaplin** 1889–
Seeking an identity

films induced the Americans to raid their music-halls for comedians and flood the world with the short comic film.

The decline of French cinema began for reasons other than war. It was stated earlier that the popular movie only survives by lapping up the new ideas dreamed up by the non-conformists. The conformist-ridden French industry grew weak from a new kind of famine which in our time threatens television: the short superficial film entertainments of the time squandered ideas, creating a desert of boredom. And the introduction of filmed theatre, *le film d'art*, a theatre without voice or depth, failed to entertain. The war effort conscripted manpower and diverted materials from the ailing French industry and the rising American industry, not involved in the war until 1917, seized the chance to fill the vacuum.

In place of the theatre piece, *le film d'art*, came the naturalist picture, the

16

**Charles Chaplin** 1889–
The identity. *City Lights* (1931)

film of the people in their streets and homes. Here exaggeration of performance was plainly inappropriate and yet underplaying was inexpressive when the human figure was far enough away to be seen at full height. With great daring the camera was moved closer to the player and personality began to count.

Up till now the shifting of the camera had only been a form of linkage from background to background and had had no dramatic effect in itself. But shifting within the scene, fragmentation of the field of view, introduced visual emphasis which was a new element in dramatization. The rhythm and tempo of the action in the field of view could be intensified and syncopated at will. And instead of linkage from scene to scene, a collision of shot against shot could be contrived amounting sometimes to shock.

The man who did most to exploit these new possibilities was the American, D. W. Griffith, who saw on the screen the effects which Europeans were achieving, often for convenience, and had the imagination to put them to positive service in dramatizing his own subjects. Griffith came to cinema in 1908 as a failed playwright and minor actor, was given an opportunity to direct, built up a devoted stock company, and in 1913 rebelled against the Trust[1] that was trying to keep the American film short and cheap, and embarked on the effort to raise the standing of cinema to the level of theatre. The result was the most outrageously and controversially successful film in history, *The Birth of a Nation* (1914), a passionate recall from his childhood of the atmosphere of the South during and after the war between the States.

Until this time most films were narrative and anecdotal, particular accounts of episodes or information on people, places, and processes. In *The Birth of a Nation* Griffith followed several threads of narrative, the friendly families in the North and South, political events in Washington, warfare with friends on opposite sides, and subsequently the exploitation of the defeated South, white and black, by carpet-baggers and thugs from the North and the rise of the Ku Klux Klan to defend the Southern whites and the friendly Negroes from extermination. He intercut these threads in a deliberately explosive manner.

One particular innovation Griffith made was in his handling of military

[1] Founded 1 January 1909, the Motion Picture Patents Company was an association of seven major American and the American branches of two French production concerns (Edison, Biograph, Vitagraph, Essanay, Kalem, Lubin, Selig, and Pathé and Star Film, the Méliès company), which collectively leased sixteen basic Edison patents and the exclusive rights to Eastman Kodak film. It came to be known as the Edison Trust and led to law-suits and physical violence provoked by the independent concerns which continued to operate. In 1910 the Trust was reconstituted as the General Film Corporation, which was finally wound up in 1919.

17

action. In this he developed the principle, which has since been too often ignored at the loss of instant understanding, of invariably keeping one group of combatants on one and the same side of the screen and the opposing force invariably on the other side; however often the position of the camera might be changed, he would never shoot from a reverse angle so as to shift a combatant from one side of the screen to the other. Even when shooting from behind an army, he would preserve the relationship of left against right and right against left. When this rule is disobeyed, the action becomes confused. Uniforms make individuals hard to recognize, and when uniforms are unfamiliar it is often a strain to tell army from army. Griffith's approach to such problems was to use a plain austere style in his aim for clarity.

When one sees this film more than fifty years later, one has to account for its *naïveté* by remembering that the lack of sensitivity in the chemicals in the emulsion of the monochromatic film dictated the limits within which the film-maker could operate. It was not a matter of Griffith's wanting to choose girls of fifteen as his leading ladies. He was forced into this policy by the physical nature of the film stock which could make a pleasing photographic image only with smooth open-faced teenagers. The girls had to pad themselves to make their figures appear adult. By the time their figures were fully developed, their faces on the screen on monochromatic stock were already assuming the look of the *femme fatale*; by twenty-five they were regarded as character actresses, by forty as grandmothers. Adult performances were beyond the inexperienced reach of youth. Only the surface of things could be explored, hence the cult of melodrama. Achievement was only possible in the simplest story-telling. Subtlety and the complications and conflicts of human relationships were unattainable.

In exploiting the personality of the player through judicious shifting of the camera, Griffith did much to found the star system. At the same time he drew so much attention to his own skill as a dramatic visualizer that the film-maker became a greater draw than the actor. If he had maintained this position even for one more film, he would have achieved for the author of a film the standing of the poet, novelist, or composer and the players would have remained his materials. But in his next film *Intolerance* (1916) Griffith pressed too ambitiously ahead for American audiences as yet scarcely affected by war, and the result was disaster.

The controversial reception of the film, *The Birth of a Nation*, which had cost the unheard of sum of 110,000 dollars, brought in a profit of 20,000,000 dollars over the next twenty years in spite of its being banned in most of the Southern States and attacked by the liberals. The experience shocked the naïve Griffith who had imagined that this interpretation of his family's experience would be accepted as truth. But his success as a film-maker brought him fame beyond any that a film-star could achieve. Creatively he saw himself as a victim of intolerance and he set himself to make a film of this idea, to illustrate four variations, examples of the idea, switching from one to another just as he had alternated the threads of narrative in his previous film.

While his associates were launching *The Birth of a Nation*, he had already made *The Mother and the Law*. This was a modern story based on a recent case about a working man condemned unjustly to death and his wife's efforts to gain a reprieve (one law for the rich and another for the poor). Two other examples of intolerance that he chose were the crucifixion of Christ and the massacre of the Huguenots on St. Bartholomew's Day. Then by *folie de grandeur* he fell for the story of Belshazzar's feast and the sack of Babylon by Cyrus the Persian, in visualizing which any hint of intolerance was swamped by a spectacle which satisfied even his envy of Italian epics like *Quo Vadis?* and *Cabiria*. For one shot he set up a camera and ordered the field of view to be filled with advancing soldiers. When the job was done, he had to pay 16,000 men. Only a totalitarian régime can pay for this kind of effusion nowadays.

In the end he had to reassemble *The Mother and the Law* and *The Fall of Babylon* as separate films to help pay his debts. For him the times were out of joint. Dramatizing an idea was too much for him, and the interweaving of four variations on an idea was ahead of the comprehension of his audience.

The repercussions were widespread. In America financiers ceased to regard the film-makers as the king-pins of production and decided to build up the film-stars in their place, putting control in the hands of the producer, aided by his cabinet of organizers and writers. This came to be known as the Hollywood system.[1]

By withholding confidence from the individual and creative film-maker, the controllers of finance dropped the *film* in favour of the *movie* tailored to the personality of the popular players whose names became more important than the titles of their pictures: they were the stars, gods and goddesses reincarnated every few months in a new role which could never be allowed to disguise their personality. Acting was out of place and make-believe took over: versatility could make stars unrecognizable and therefore valueless.

Making commercially successful *movies* meant inventing variations on chosen themes, the themes being embodied in the cinegenic personalities of stars. It was an ambiguous pursuit, a combination of cold-blooded calculation

[1] In reaction, the three leading American stars, Chaplin, Fairbanks, and Pickford joined with Griffith to control their own production and distribution, forming the United Artists Corporation in 1919, cutting out the middle-men whose techniques of survival have always been unerring.

**D. W. Griffith**
1875–1948
Between takes, with eye-shield
ready

and psychological insight, of private and public relations, as these valuable investments grew older in private, clinging all the while to their youth in public. If the resulting *movies* had any relationship with life, it was a coincidence without meaning to the promoters. Synthetic myth, artificial mystery, and the daylight carefully filtered. The real was disguised under the cosmetic, just as nature was blunted by censorship.

Yet the failure of *Intolerance* did more to advance the development of cinema than the success of a myriad of conventional films. These were usually composed of elements which prompted the heresy that described cinema as a language:[1] long-shot, mid-shot, close-up, and their intermediate variants. The habit was, in the jargon of the time, to cover (or film) so many pages of the shooting script by making a long-shot of all the action contained in that section; then to move the camera forward and break up the action into a number of mid-shots (pairs of actors) or single close-ups for climactic moments and reactions. In this way a *metteur-en-scène* could send to the cutting-room film which in fact variously covered the action described in the script three or four times. Out of this variety the editor, with or without supervision by producer or director, could evolve a balanced visualization of the script, choosing shots for emphasis, slowing down or speeding up the action to taste, often eliminating a dull scene and sometimes using suggestion rather than statement to excite the imagination of the audience.[2]

But the *réalisateur*, a real film-maker like Griffith, would prove that this humdrum method of adopting a language was anathema. An example from *The Birth of a Nation*: in a shot half-way between close and mid-shot a mother and children cower behind a hedge and then the camera pans (makes a panoramic movement) to the other side of the hedge where down below in long-shot in the valley General Sherman's troops are marching past a house in ruins on their way to Atlanta. A 'language' script would make this action into two shots, a mid-shot and a long-shot. Yet it is the linking movement that dramatizes the scene.

Griffith saw his film in his mind before he began. His powers of suggestion

[1] It was the French who first described cinema as a *langage*. The heresy arose out of the mistranslation of the word as 'language'. The French word for language is *langue*. *Langage* means speech, a way of speaking. *Le langage du cinéma* means a visual way of telling a story or making a statement: the phrase was never intended to lead to a study of grammar and syntax.

[2] Until the invention of lavender (1929) and later of fine grain (1940) positive film from which duplicate negatives are made, it was customary to shoot more than one adequate performance of every camera set-up, so that two versions (home and export) of the film could be assembled in the cutting-room. If sales demanded more copies than could be printed from two negatives, a third negative was assembled which often varied from the original if insufficient or inadequate identical material remained. Film archivists are sometimes puzzled by variations in early films and try to trace which version comes from the original first negative.

**Erich von Stroheim** 1885–1957
D.W.G.'s link with the
narrative stream

**Sergei M. Eisenstein** 1898–1948
D.W.G.'s link with the film of
ideas

are still valid. When the soldier son returns wounded and in rags to the southern family home now decrepit, his little sister greets him at the gate and leads him to the porch. The front door is at an oblique angle and not seen, nor is the mother. Only her arms come out of the doorway and gather him into the house: literally, this example of synecdoche is corny, but even after fifty years the scene is still visually moving. And what have words got to do with it? The best of cinema, like music, is usually indescribable in words. The impact of film is instantaneous while literature to build up a picture has to use one damn word after another, over a period of seconds.

Griffith made innumerable experiments in the 400 shorter films that he executed before *The Birth of a Nation* and less and less of them had any connection with literature and drama. It was he who began the cinematic juggling with tempo, altering the speed of the camera according to the mood of the action. In love scenes he speeded it up so that in projection the scene would play more slowly. In moments of tense action, he would suddenly change by cutting from slow to fast. In a workers' dance in *Intolerance* the gaiety is emphasized by the slow turning of the camera, cranked by hand, which increased the tempo when the scene was projected at normal speed. In cinemas on Saturdays and holidays it became the custom to project the silent programmes, the machine again cranked by hand, so much faster that there was time for an additional performance during the day. One of the assets of the silent film was the habit of projecting it slightly faster than life, and the early sound films were often accused of dullness because cameras and projectors had to be cranked by motors locked at the same constant speed. The silent film was certainly a freer and therefore to purists a more exacting medium than the early sound film which was enslaved to inadequate machinery.

Griffith's subsequent career was devoted to paying off all his debts, and his comparative standing among his rivals as a film-maker in America was no less honourable until the coming of sound. His failing was that he lacked the third eye, the eye that vigilantly watches the prospect from afar while the other two are intent on immediate business.

All Griffith's assistants became directors and the greatest called himself Erich von Stroheim. As he developed, his films brought his backers prestige and profit until he too shot ahead of his time and made in 1923 a masterpiece *Greed* of which the distributors allowed the world to see only a mutilated version of less than half its intended length. He was a perfectionist who built his films in the camera in the manner accepted nowadays in the era which I call Phase Three.

Audaciously he rejected Griffith's method of invariably confronting the

21

passive spectator with the simple image that Griffith chose as suitable for him: instead he often left to the spectator the choice of selecting in a complex image of longer duration the action he preferred to follow. Thus the spectator is given freedom of choice, of activity, is invited to use his intelligence as well as to indulge his emotions, even to see the film more than once in order to discover further riches. Stroheim was too subtle to leave selection, emphasis, and timing wholly to the cutting-room, though he let no one else assemble his work so long as he was allowed to keep control. If he had been able to use the wide screen of today, the cinema would now be a more exciting place.

Stroheim used the deep focus capacity of orthochromatic film creatively. In his satires of the romantic (his Ruritanian black comedies) he used the resources of the film studio. But in *Greed*, with its reflections of contemporary California, he quit the studio and worked entirely on the locations described in Frank Norris's novel *McTeague* which was the basis of his film. Typical of his approach is the comic wedding in the dental parlour with a funeral procession passing in sharp focus in the street below. For the climactic sequence in Death Valley, he worked in the valley itself, committing some of his unit to hospital. Neither sound, colour, smell, nor third dimension, nor the positive style of editing known as montage, are needed: what is on the film is enough for the imaginative audience.

Stroheim was the first of the mature film-makers, a singularly difficult man, whose temperament, egotistic, stubborn, witty, uncompromising, was utterly inappropriate to fit into the Hollywood industry which he dubbed the sausage machine: to them he embodied anathema. He never completed a sound film and earned his subsequent living as an actor of uncommon intelligence. Even today there are writers who do not appreciate Stroheim's attitude to his audience, an attitude prevalent in the third phase of cinema.

But before we move on to further phases, we have to consider Eisenstein, the Russian master, and his methods of montage.

It is ironical that one so politically naïve and melodramatically inclined as Griffith should have inspired both the sophisticated entertainer, Stroheim, and the intellectual Eisenstein and through him the whole development of the film of persuasion. Stroheim, Renoir, neo-realism, and the *nouvelle vague* on the one hand, and Eisenstein, documentary, and propaganda on the other.

By a quirk of history a copy of *Intolerance* reached Berlin in March 1917 only to be impounded next month as enemy property, when the U.S.A. declared war on Germany. After the war the German communist International Workers' Aid smuggled the film among a steady flow of foodstuffs and medical supplies across the blockaded frontier into the Soviet Union where it was studied with admiration as a work of cinema and was censored into communist approval by Esther Shub. Later, after the raising of the blockade in 1920, a copy of *The Birth of a Nation* reached Moscow. In 1923 Lenin sent a trade delegation to the U.S.A. and with it a letter inviting Griffith to take charge of film production in the Russian republic. But he turned down the offer. However, his two films had shown Eisenstein the way to his discovery that the film can do more than relate the particular anecdote, that it can generalize as well.

Eisenstein loyally supported the Bolshevik Revolution but he was never a Communist Party member. Born in Riga in 1898 of bourgeois stock, ignored by his parents and tied nearly all his life to the apron-strings of his old peasant nanny, he longed to share and understand the life of the workers and peasants, but it all came to him at second-hand. He joined the Red Army, worked in it as a cartoon poster artist and on demobilization joined the Proletkult Theatre to qualify for a civilian ration card in the most congenial way available. As a designer he took a particular interest in environment and when the theatre was found wanting, he even put on a play (*Gas Masks*) in a factory, staging the action among the machines which were the background of the drama. But the factory proved to be too untheatrical, too awkward. In search of dramatic realism he filmed one of the scenes for his forthcoming stage production. And following this, he took the plunge. For his next assignment he made the Proletkult Theatre into a cinema.

Eisenstein turned to cinema in 1924 when in Russia film production was at its lowest ebb; leading professionals had fled years ago to the West, equipment was worn out and film stock exhausted. The coherent films available were largely capitalist and film-makers like Esther Shub were forced to strip them down and reassemble them with new sub-titles and occasionally with new scenes, compatible with the new socialist order. It was an exciting moment when there was nothing to lose and everything to gain from experiment. Out of their efforts the compilation film was born, the film which finds new meaning in the fresh arrangement of shots made for a totally different purpose.

For his first original film Eisenstein took his players out of the theatre and made *Strike* (1924). In this picture Eisenstein compared the action of cavalry quelling a strike of workers with that of butchers slaughtering livestock, much to the disapproval of purists who claim that symbolism should derive from the elements of the story being narrated and should not be dragged in arbitrarily from sources separate from the story.

Eisenstein and his successors learnt from this mistake, just as he learnt from the errors in Griffith's *Intolerance*. In this film Griffith had used as a recurring symbol binding together the threads of his four stories a long shot of Lilian Gish sitting on a chair placidly rocking a cradle on the floor beside her while three old women sit motionless in the background. For Griffith this meant the life force persisting in spite of the intolerance and inhumanity of mankind. To Eisenstein and the rest of the world it represented a young woman rocking a cradle. Why was it particular when Griffith intended it as a generalization? Eisenstein believed that a detail of the scene, for example the mother's hand clasping the baby's hand, by epitomizing the whole scene would in doing so imply the continuity of life. While the cameraman described the shot as a close-up, which is a geographic expression, Eisenstein regarded it as a symbolic detail. From then on practically every shot he composed (and he had a masterly eye for a composition) represented a physical intention and suggested an idea as well, if you wanted to look for it. In fitting his shots together one after the other he had both purposes in mind, so that the collision of shot with shot added significance to the meaning behind each. When he was lecturing to the Film Society study group in London in 1930, I remember asking him in my capacity as a film-editor, if he ever made a smooth cut from shot to shot so as to be almost imperceptible, which was the style beloved of current film entertainers, and he replied: no, that would be a shocking waste of an opportunity.[1] He transcended Griffith's method of shepherding his passive audience along a chosen line of narrative. He used shock tactics in the selection of his material, confronting his audience with images of such symbolic content that they were forced to keep their wits sharpened and to participate in the scenes set before them. Here was propaganda that stimulated: it left the intelligent spectator convinced or enraged but never indifferent. But as his work became more intricate following the success of *The Battleship Potemkin* (1925), his approach left the Soviet public stone cold. However, Berlin, sated with the theatricality of a cinema dominated by the disciples of Max Reinhardt and still shaken by the nightmare of recent inflation[2] and incipient Nazism, rose to the films of Eisenstein, and the rest of Europe followed suit so far as political censorship allowed. *The Battleship Potemkin* was acclaimed as flawless. In *Old and New* (1929) he tried with satire and some audacity to break down the conservatism of the peasants in favour of collectivization. But the content was strange to foreigners and to nationals the style was alien. His greatest innovation was his experiment in intellectual cinema *October* (1928). The first half of this immense film is like a

[1] Eisenstein's experiments in montage derived from necessity. Shortage of negative made every scrap of 'short end' worth its weight in gold. Two shots would take the place of one, but often a new concept flowered from the juxtaposition of shot against shot.

[2] In August 1922, 8500 marks = £1; in August 1923, 20 million marks; in October 1924, 19 million million marks = £1 (i.e., nearly four million million marks to the U.S. dollar).

great sprawling live cartoon. It seemed, too, that Eisenstein lacked, as much as Griffith, that third eye of calculating professionalism. But he was also beset by current events, a bauble in an erratic flood. He accepted the commission to make this impression of the October 1917 revolution for the tenth anniversary celebrations when *Old and New* was already in production. Even with the devoted collaboration of his associate, Grigori Alexandrov, controlling a second unit, he was unable to achieve the ambitions of his conception and was forced to skimp the second half of the film. By the time of the first public screening, three months late, Trotsky, a leading figure with Lenin ten years before, had fallen from power and every close shot of him save one had had to be torn out of the film as if he had never participated in the revolution.

So this is not a work of art for the aesthete but for those who love cinema, warts and all, those who are not afraid to grip and handle cinema, the film, often blundering and shapeless and over-emphatic, contains peak after peak of satire and irony. You cannot fathom all that has been discovered in cinema without studying the successes and the failures of this film and without knowing the history and sociology both of its subject and of the time, ten years later, when it was made. *October* is a wicked reflection of those times.

A more concise version of the film was assembled in Berlin under the title borrowed from John Reed's diary of these events *Ten Days that Shook the World* (1928), and it proved sensational enough for a New York impresario to prepare it for release in a Broadway theatre. But by the time it was ready America had lost interest in the silent film and *October* was never shown publicly in America in any form until the present time.

From Eisenstein's silent films, his pursuit of persuasion through generalization and symbolism, was derived the whole school miscalled 'documentary', 'the creative interpretation of reality', as John Grierson defined it. Since this concept is a matter of opinion, the term documentary has become so debased as to be meaningless: it is now applied to any factual film, even one that describes a mechanical process.

One has sympathy for the need for pigeon-holes or categories, but if one is forced to adopt them one should determine them by facts, not opinions. Surely a factual film should be realistic, a sober reconstruction as true to life as is reasonable. None of Eisenstein's work was wholly factual, for example in *Potemkin* he never intended to stage a sequence on the Odessa Steps until he went location hunting and found them. Whereupon they so fired his imagination that poetically he was able to distil an impression more vivid and compelling than anything that took place in real life in Odessa during the 1905 Revolution. If you measure the steps and the speed of the soldiers' descent, you find that Eisenstein spun out the event to three or four times the length of time that would have been taken if the event had really happened. This is certainly an extension of the creative interpretation of reality in the most generous sense and it is an insult to put it in the same pigeon-hole as a demonstration of how to change a tyre on the wheel of a motor-car.

The difference lies in the capacity of the film-maker. Factual films can be made by skilled cinematographers, cameramen. The *Delhi Durbar of 1911* was made in an early two-colour system, Kinemacolor, by a cameraman. Herbert Ponting, alone with one camera, filmed the Scott Polar Expedition of 1912. Newsreel cameramen contributed to the reportage films of the world wars. All they needed in addition to their photographic skill was a sense of continuity, of lining up shot to follow shot, and a skilled editor to graft it all together. The event was dominant either as it happened or in reconstruction and whatever did not reflect the event was irrelevant. The same principle covers the description of a mechanical process. The layman often imagines that the one member of a film unit who can be dispensed with or replaced by a layman is the director. The fact is that in situations where direction is not dominant, the function of direction can be undertaken by another member of the unit. There are situations where the photographic demands are so meagre that an assistant cameraman, or even the director himself, can fulfil them. But the relevant function has to be undertaken by someone and the more exacting the subject the more skill is needed.

The function of film making can be described as a pole, which at the less exacting end merges with the working of the camera and at the more exacting end involves the artist. The results stretch from the accurate record of actuality to the deep exploration of the human condition.

Among Eisenstein's Soviet contemporaries one, Dziga Vertov, began by insisting on staging nothing, on having no action repeated for the benefit of his camera: his aim was to catch life unawares. For him the lens was an eye not to be insulted by pseudo-events. But he found it increasingly hard to reveal anything behind the surface of reality: he was like a composer who confines himself to one melodic line, and later he turned to trickery within the camera including the animation of still pictures and photographing the camera moving like a robot seeking some object of interest. It became a tedious exercise until the coming of sound which gave him the means to comment on his visual records. In his work lurks the embryo of *cinéma vérité* to which we shall come in discussing the third phase of cinema.

While Eisenstein and Vertov were communicating first to the intelligence in order to stir the emotions, the rest of their contemporaries were following the more orthodox line of appealing to the emotions direct, content to dramatize the particular anecdote. Among them two remain outstanding, the better

**Vsevolod Pudovkin**
1892–1940
From science to narrative

**Alexander Dovzhenko**
1894–1956
The silent poet

known Pudovkin, the less known Dovzhenko. Pudovkin—student of chemistry, sharp, flexible, nimble, highly professional—gauged his audience invariably and was able to bend his convictions to every twist and turn of the party line. Dovzhenko—peasant and painter—expressed himself without compromise, inflexibly, and with consummate beauty. It is typical of him that when his party membership card was lost in the post and never reached him, he refused to claim another because to do so meant signing a confession of having lost the card himself.

Another great innovator in the Lumière tradition, working on the other side of the world, was the American liberal romantic Robert Flaherty. Driven from Ireland like millions more by the potato famine of the 1860s, Flaherty's father became a mining engineer in America only to be deprived a second time by the economic crisis of 1893. Young Flaherty grew up first in an atmosphere of industrial unrest and subsequently of pioneering in the wilds of Canada. He became more interested in exploring than in mining and in discovering personality than in uncovering objects. But the only way to share such discoveries was to film them. His first film *Nanook of the North* (1921), a masterly study of an Eskimo hunter and his family, was backed by the furriers Revillon Frères and led in 1923 to a Paramount contract to make a Nanook of the south seas.

Flaherty was one of the rare complete film-makers who even processed his own negative unaided when he worked in remote locations. This is how he stumbled on the innovation which was to revolutionize the motion picture almost as much as the introduction of sound. For he undertook also to make a colour film in a new additive colour system called Prizmacolor,[1] alongside the feature film that came to be called *Moana* (1926) and which was to be shot in black and white with the conventional orthochromatic negative. Prizmacolor was produced in a special camera, equipped with alternating colour filters and using panchromatic, an improved black and white negative sensitive to all colours. Orthochromatic film had produced splendid results in the strong dark and light aspects of the far north but it proved disappointing in recording the multi-colours of a south sea island. And the golden skins of the Polynesians appeared almost negroid.

Fortunately the colour camera broke down and Flaherty made a test on panchromatic negative using one of his Akeley black and white cameras. The result was so beautiful that he sent for enough panchromatic stock to shoot

[1] The additive processes, in short, consist of black and white images sensitive to all colours photographed and projected through two or three colour filters. This system came to be superseded, inevitably, by the subtractive processes which end up with a coloured positive print which is projected in the ordinary way.

**Robert Flaherty**
1884–1951

## LONE FILM-MAKERS

**Alberto Cavalcanti**
1897–

the whole film in black and white and entirely abandoned the colour film project.

Flaherty was not merely the right man in the right place. He was the only living film-maker who could take such a chance. When *Moana* was finally screened in Hollywood in 1925, orthochromatic film was doomed.

However, as I mentioned earlier, in abandoning the harsh orthochromatic in favour of the more subtle panchromatic, film-making lost the range of focus which had been the great asset of its early days. Film-makers had to decide where to set their focus and in making an apparent virtue out of necessity they lost the constant presence of background, of environment, that had lain at the heart of cinema. By coincidence the sound-track was just being introduced, and its intelligent use could do something to suggest the missing element. But most of the time the necessary intelligence was missing. Another stage in the erratic progress of cinema had been reached.

At the same time as Eisenstein and his contemporaries in the Soviet Union were scanning the Lumière line, the living picture, to its furthest extremities as a weapon of socialism, in Germany the pendulum of cinema swung in the opposite direction, that of the Méliès or theatrical school: from outdoors to hothouse, daylight to arc light. And from far left to far right in politics. Of the parties in Germany responsible for defeat in 1918 only the Kaiser fled the country. Big business consolidated itself under government intervention. The effect in cinema was to filter into the industry ideas and artists of right-wing tendencies. The leftist film-writer Carl Mayer to earn his living was forced to reverse the intention of subjects of his like *The Cabinet of Dr. Caligari* (1919) and *The Last Laugh* (1924) from antagonism to commendation of the capitalist establishment. To *Caligari* the producer, Erich Pommer, tacked on a prologue and epilogue which showed that this attack on authority and its abuses was the invention of a madman, that the apparently villainous Doctor was in fact a wise and good man. In *The Last Laugh* tragedy was averted when a millionaire capriciously left his fortune to the crumbling old lavatory attendant, hence justifying the English translation of the original German title *Der letzte Mann*. It was in this atmosphere that big business took advantage of the inflation to make spectacular films at a comparatively low cost which would have meant slave rates of pay in any other country and which they were able to sell all over the world at a vast profit. In Germany the returns were negligible and many fewer films were made for local consumption than before. The Germans also were the first to cater for the minority 'art house' audience by making highly theatrical 'chamber films' of exotic dramas with few sets and at small cost. Theatricality came naturally to them as they drew on the writers, directors, and designers trained by Max Rein-

**Carl Mayer**
1892–1944
Austrian writer

**F. W. Murnau**
1888–1931
German director

hardt who was reigning supreme over the German theatre as a kind of Minister of National Diversion to boost the people's morale. The resulting 'hothouse' films in no way competed with the outdoor, down-to-earth entertainments provided from Hollywood: instead they complemented them. When in October 1924 the Americans, by stabilizing the German currency at nineteen marks to the pound sterling, incidentally forced up the costs of all German products to the international level, the German film industry began to dwindle and Hollywood fertilized its own last period of silent cinema by luring the cream of German talent to California. The marriage of Berlin with Hollywood is typified in William Fox's exuberant production *Sunrise* (1927), written by Carl Mayer from Hermann Sudermann's story *The Journey to Tilsit*, directed by F. W. Murnau, designed by Rochus Gliese (all from Berlin), photographed by Karl Struss and Charles Rosher (both American), and played by a typical Hollywood cast. The film is an epitome of the German formal approach transferred to the open air and the surface reality which allows the audience to identify with the action in the American manner. Murnau was a great admirer of Robert Flaherty's work and *Sunrise*[1] was among the first major commercial pictures to be photographed on panchromatic negative. The result was remarkable even to the layman.

This golden age of the German cinema served the best of both worlds: it acknowledged and reflected the conditions which ripen revolution while asserting that every cloud has a silver lining and all will come right in the end. Design and craftsmanship were imaginative and highly professional and the stylization of expressionism rampant in the theatre were translated into terms of cinema boldly and consistently. Unreality in décor, lighting, costume, make-up, and performance created new environments that at the time made sense as silent cinema, but the movement could not have survived in the sound film where stylized dialogue spoken with a similar lack of reality would have provoked total disbelief. And few of these German silent films with their over-emphatic playing appear believable today: the moving pictures are often admirable but one cannot accept the exaggerations of their illusion.

Indeed the German contribution to the advance of cinema has always been one of design. There is a term 'storyboard', almost wholly a matter of design. The storyboard is the 'script' visualized by drawings of every basic change of camera angles in the film. The Germans were the first to apply this system to the living picture and their designers later carried this notion to America, Britain, and elsewhere. Films like *Gone with the Wind* (1939) and *Things to Come* (1936) were entirely preconceived on the drawing-board and *metteurs-*

[1] Carl Dreyer used panchromatic negative in France in 1928 on *The Passion of Joan of Arc.* Jean Renoir was using it at the same time.

*en-scène* were forced to set up their cameras so that the field of view of each shot was a mimicry of the designer's intention. Thus a marked proportion of the function of direction was transferred to the designer unless the director had the time and permission to collaborate in the design.[1]

The Russians had the right idea when they paid due attention to composition by carrying an impression of the finished film in their mind and adapting it to their surroundings in the execution of their ideas. And the rest of the world has always come back to this method however often they have tried something different. But the Germans would not renounce the example of the theatre: they had to have a precedent from which to advance thought by thought. They were justified by the hideous reality around them at the time in trying to invent illusions that were in joint, but these sickroom methods are invalid in a more healthy world.

The German preoccupation with design led them to introduce that ponderous method of visual punning that, for instance, shows the passage of time by tracking for no apparent reason towards a candle flame and dissolving to a lighted gas jet or electric bulb from which inevitably they track away to the next sequence in their story. This nudging of the audience was mercifully superseded by the exponents of the *nouvelle vague* who, sated with early cinema, learnt to jump from period to period without warning of any kind. But they had to be sated first. In Germany the same preoccupation led to the formality of their attitude to the factual film which they dubbed 'Kultur-Film'. Here their visual punning has sometimes reached wit, making bearable the geographical 'travelogue' which in Anglo-American cinema is known as the 'and-so-we-say-farewell' school. But there is no need to torture ourselves further in this direction.

While Europe was involved in the First World War, which lasted more than four years and cost more than 10,000,000 lives with twice as many more victims of the epidemics that followed, the U.S.A. suffered six months of active combat on foreign soil with 115,000 dead. An industrial and trade boom developed, lasting ten years, and the film played a big part in the drive for foreign sales. Indeed, the slogan 'Trade Follows the Film' was no myth. When on the screen a film-star removed his shirt and revealed his torso, the vest or undershirt went out of fashion; if he used a safety razor, sales of the cut-throat razor dwindled. Because a big proportion of the audience sits on the side, rather than in the middle, of the auditorium, their view of the screen

[1] The artificiality of this approach was carried to a dead-end of absurdity in Britain in the late 1940s, with the introduction (and rapid abandonment) of the *independent frame*, a system which gave absolute control to the function of design on grounds of economy. The result was a total absence of the freedom to improvise which in the current third phase of cinema has become recognized as vital.

is distorted and the image appears narrower: the slimmer image introduced the fashion for slimming the human figure. Marlene Dietrich started the craze of trousers for women by her cool aplomb in wearing them on the screen.

The British film had a modest reputation before the First World War and gained in stature with the factual war records which the Government exported as propaganda. But, as elsewhere, the Americans took over the British market, selling their product not singly but in 'blocks' often before completion. By 1925 the Government was scared when modestly the British producers asked that cinemas should be encouraged to show one British programme per year. In 1927 block booking was forbidden by law and a 5% quota was introduced, but the Americans wrecked this by surreptitiously agreeing among themselves not to pay more than one pound sterling for any foot of film that they were forced to buy to fill their distribution quota and to keep such films to the shortest length—6000 feet—required by law. Apart from the films the Americans made in Britain themselves, these 'quota quickies'[1] were produced for them by British companies under contract for £6000 each. Their quality was dismal. To discredit British films further the American-owned cinemas would fulfil the letter of the law by arbitrarily cutting these films, making what began as dull into an insulting illogicality. Or more mercifully they would show them uncut in the mornings while the cleaners were still at work. There was a brain-drain to Hollywood for any who could show ability in this colonial situation. But 'quota quickies' were a mockery of a training ground for young film-makers, since they had to be made in imitation of the Hollywood studio-built film and usually that meant five days on the studio floor. Two hopeful signs emerged from this depressing situation: the early work of Alfred Hitchcock and the first silent factual efforts of the Empire Marketing Board film unit under John Grierson to coax some export trade.

For some of the more forward looking the coming of radio broadcasting in the early 1920s exposed the basic deficiency, the silence, of cinema. However, the financiers argued that until the silent film had reached saturation point in the world markets it would not decline since there was no language barrier apart from the minimal cost of translating sub-titles. In an effort to prevent

[1] During the prosperous 1920s the American drugstore would refill your coffee cup free of charge. They called this the 'twofer' (two for the price of one) and they adopted the habit in cinema performances by showing two feature (or long) films for the price of one. Then they began making cheaper pictures (B pictures) to accompany the main (A) feature. They introduced the system to the British market and offered the 'quota quickie' as the B picture. The double-feature system has remained obstinately prevalent ever since and has banished the individual short film from circulation in popular cinemas in Britain and America, other than the news, magazine, and cartoon films available in series. In all other countries the single-feature programme prevails and with it the short film is encouraged.

the decline in established markets meanwhile, Hollywood imported talent particularly from Europe to exploit every possible innovation in visual ingenuity. But dissatisfaction permeated the mass audience to such an extent that by 1927 the producers were facing disaster.

Lack of a sound-track made it almost impossible to reveal anything beneath the surface of the image either in characterization or comment. The popular film was content to illustrate a simple story. Each new sequence began with a narrative title rounding off the point of the sequence before and blatantly describing the action that was to follow. It was the comics with their capers and the Westerns with their landscapes and their shocks, all stated with speed and clarity, that appealed to the discriminating as well as to the mass audience. There was irony in the fact that the quality of the comic and the Western derives from their remoteness from 'front office' control, the dead hand of finance. Westerns were made on locations at a distance from the studio. Comic films were woven around, and often by, the talent of a comic actor or a team of comedians. Once a production of either of these types began, it was useless for the controllers of finance to interfere. And when the comedian was a keen businessman as well, he was able to finance his own productions out of his profits as his own distributor. This is not the place to recount the fabulous history of Dr. Charles Chaplin, that obstinate English pearl in the Hollywood oyster. He was eventually banished thence by his all-round non-conformity, surviving long enough to pass through Phase Two, the early period of the sound film, with honours, having given to the country of his adoption as much as, or more than, he had ever taken from it. His work amply rewards close examination since it demonstrates that in the expression of comic action, clarity and bareness of style are of paramount importance.

Some critics thought that Chaplin was incapable of a more personal style of direction. Then in 1923 as Stroheim was finishing *Greed*, Chaplin rewarded his leading lady of the time, Edna Purviance, by starring her in *A Woman of Paris* (a film in which he himself did not appear), a serious, social study in which, as far as one's memory allows, he demonstrated new ways of using suggestion and ambiguity which added a totally unsuspected dimension to the reputation of the most widely recognized entertainer in history.

It is greatly to be hoped that sooner or later the complete works of this master will be made available for study. They have suffered more piracy and are therefore more jealously guarded than any other films. His work runs a gamut from crude music-hall knockabout, through sharp, cruel derision, to social comment and a tendency to overdo sentimentality. Chaplin had many rivals in the field of silent comedy, Buster Keaton, Harold Lloyd, Harry

Langdon, W. C. Fields, and others, but none could surpass his pathos and the implication of social comment that enriches his work.

Apart from the great merit which the discriminating found in the work of Chaplin and his contemporaries in American comedy and indeed in the American Western films, there was also their originality. These films were almost exclusively conceived in terms of cinema, not derived from works of literature and drama, the source of the bulk of film entertainment. They were not 'photographs of something else'. Described in words they would lose meaning, as so many have discovered in coming home from the pictures and trying to explain what they are laughing at. This is the element that fired the *avant-garde*: originality, which the conservative often found startling and therefore considered vulgar. While the conservative could stomach films of geographical expeditions and silent versions of established novels and dramas, the *avant-garde* started supporting the unusual original film.

In Britain there began to emerge recognition of the *film* as opposed to the *movie* in 1925 when Ivor Montagu organized in London The Film Society for the study of films unavailable through normal channels of distribution.

The film society movement began tentatively in Paris in 1920 when Ricciotto Canudo founded his club The Friends of the Seventh Art, and again in 1922 when the critic and *réalisateur* Louis Delluc founded his Ciné-Club. Neither prospered for long. Then in 1924 Charles Léger started the first regular film society The Free Tribune of Cinema and Jean Tedesco took over the small Vieux-Colombier Theatre and began the specialized cinema, or art house, movement. The new status of film was marked by advertising the starting times of programmes. Only D. W. Griffith had dared in the early days to introduce the separate performance in place of continuous performances.

Fertilized by this interest in the original film, the *avant-garde* movement began breaking the physical and mental conventions of the cinema as a mass medium. The length of a film ceased to be a criterion of its importance. The short film, less than an hour in length and sometimes lasting only a few minutes, came into its own.

For one thing, though the average cost of silent filming was low in comparison with that of shooting with sound, it took imagination as well as private means to finance experiments in cinema in the 1920s, and so length was a determining factor. It soon became clear that the shorter film was the appropriate medium for testing and training talent. And ever since, the short film has been so recognized and encouraged except in 'Ameranglian' cinema where the double-feature programme hogs the market, leaving no time for the independent short film. In all fairness, it must be emphasized that it costs as

**Jean Cocteau**
1889–1963

**WHAT IS REALITY?**

**Luis Buñuel**
1900–

much, and takes as much time and trouble to publish a short as a long film: the effort can be the same for ten minutes as for a hundred minutes of entertainment and the returns are commensurate to the length of the film, not to the effort involved. As most producers live from film to film, the longer for them the better.

The debt of the cinema to the patrons of the *avant-garde* movement is immeasurable. The lead was given, as so often, in France, where cinema was first recognized as an art. Luis Buñuel, Alberto Cavalcanti, René Clair, Jean Cocteau, Louis Delluc, Germaine Dulac, Jean Epstein, Jean Grémillon, Marcel L'Herbier, Jean Renoir, Jean Vigo, were all launched on their careers by the active support of ciné-club and art house.

Naturally in these early days the gulf between *avant-garde* and industry was much wider than it is today. Except in Moscow, there were no film schools with archives[1] where the beginner could be grounded in techniques and in the history, theory, and practice of production, distribution, and exhibition. The experience of leaving the shelter of private patronage and challenging the wide-open spaces of public entertaining was cruel and exacting. It took Luis Buñuel fourteen years of unrewarding effort to bridge the gap between his surrealist period (*Un Chien andalou* (1928), *L'Age d'or* (1930), *Land without Bread* (1932)) and his first commercial job of direction, and another four before he was allowed to make a subject of his own choice: *Los Olvidados* in 1950. His was the extreme case, but most of those who began their film work under private patronage have had to indulge in some form of worldly compromise to gain commercial backing.

Of French members of the *avant-garde*, René Clair and Jean Renoir have enjoyed among the longest and most honourable of any careers in cinema. Clair was already secure in the last days of silent film and the early years of sound, thanks to the cosmopolitan nature of the film industry in France after the First World War. Indeed, in the first twenty years of his career this embodiment of all that is French depended almost entirely on foreign promoters. A marked proportion of the foreign colony, itself a high proportion of the film world of Paris in the 1920s, was made up of refugees from the Bolshevik Revolution. It was Alexander Kamenka, a gifted Russian associate of the exiled Tsarist producer Ermolief, who produced *An Italian Straw Hat* (1927), the comic silent film which keeps the world in debt to René Clair. Paris was free from chauvinism in those days. One recalls a film unit in 1925 which involved seventeen nationalities and a babel of interpreters. But there was no

[1] The oldest film archive in the world is the specialist collection at the Imperial War Museum, London, founded in 1918. The National Film Archive was set up in 1935. Neither was able to make much provision for students.

34

trade union. Clair was to sustain French expression in the early sound film entirely with German support. Renoir was to emerge later than Clair and is now recognized as the earliest pioneer of modern cinema. We shall come to him later.

By the end of this first phase of cinema, which came in the U.S.A. in 1928, in Europe in 1929 and 1930, and in the Soviet Union in 1931, existing markets were waning faster than new markets could be found that were rich enough to compensate. There were outdoor cinemas in Africa showing silent films as late as 1936 and probably in Asia too.

The range of silent cinema was wide but shallow. Every kind of subject that exists today was available then. Even the stories of operas were shown accompanied by musical scores based on the original work and under the composer's supervision, if he were alive. *Der Rosenkavalier* (1926) was particularly successful.

But there was no depth because there was no speech, and in most cases without speech there can be no characterization except in the limited field of mime. Comedians were mimes, and a Chaplin or a Keaton could carry cinema deeper than any tragedian, even than Pauline Frederick or Sessue Hayakawa, the only Hollywood stars who were accorded the honour of an unhappy ending to their films.

The silent cinema had mastered space, but it took the sound film another thirty years to conquer time, and only by the combination of these two could human character be established in depth on the screen.

But the sound-track was introduced, not as a stimulus to the mind of cinema but wholly as a physical stunt, like the widening of the screen later on, as a desperate effort to break a log-jam, to bring back the dwindling audience into the cinema. It was desperate because no one could foresee an adequate solution to the problem of language translation which had never bothered the makers of silent film.

The banks loaned the money for the purchase of equipment but no capital was available for experiment in dramatic method. As before, film-makers had to continue to earn their living from film to film while they were exploring new techniques of entertainment. Reluctance was only overcome by the disastrous, often total, failure of the last of the silent films to get any money back at all. Sound was providing the public with a new dimension in entertainment that only the purists would deny. Ironically, many of the purists were among the *avant-garde* of the silent film, and far from contributing ideas for experiment, they scorned the sound-track as a typical Hollywood vulgarity: an opinion too often justified by the first offspring of the marriage of sight and sound.

Stroheim
**GREED**
1923
**Silent forerunner of the
modern realist film staged
in its authentic
environment**

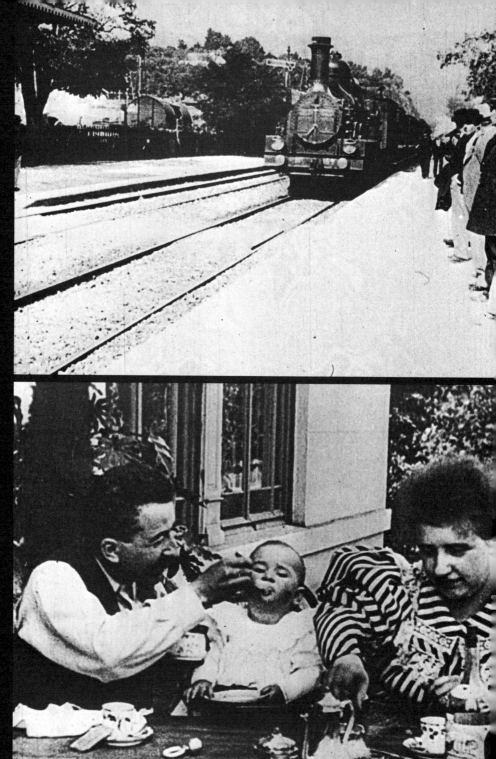

The first audiences were
disturbed by the approach of
the train

**From the first
Lumière programme**

**THE LIVING PICTURE**
1895
and enchanted by the breeze
blowing the leaves in the
garden

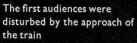

Georges Méliès
**LE VOYAGE DANS
LA LUNE**
1902
**Early science fiction**

**The Theatrical
Picture**

Giovanni Pastrone
**CABIRIA**
1913
**A sense of scale**

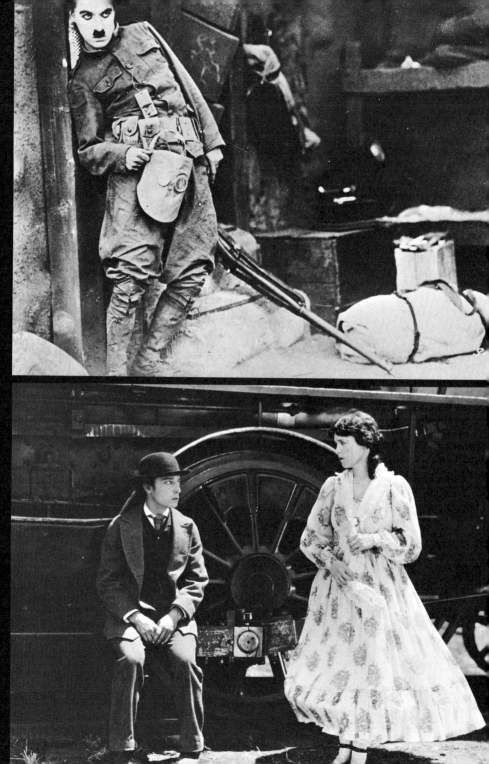

**Charles Chaplin**
**SHOULDER ARMS**
1918
This film was run as a
double bill in the Thirties
with G. W. Pabst's
*Westfront 1918* (1930).
Pabst's film with full
studio resources of its
period lacked everything
that is in *Shoulder Arms.*
The audience was involved
with Chaplin, the
conscript lost in a bloody
bureaucratic trench war.
One had to laugh or one
would have had to cry

**War as
entertainment**

**Buster Keaton**
**THE GENERAL**
1927
With Marian Mack.
Keaton arrived late in the
early cinema, a master of
charm and timing

'D. W. Griffith's mighty
spectacle. The sweetest love
story ever told. With a cast
of thousands.' Publicity line

**THE BIRTH OF A
NATION**
1914

The agonizing outcome of
civil war: a compatriot
chained by a compatriot.
President Wilson said:
'Like writing history with
lightning'

D. W. Griffith
**INTOLERANCE**
1916
Sub-titled 'Love's
Struggle Through the
Ages'

←
**THE FALL OF
BABYLON**
When run as a separate
film sub-titled: 'A Purple
Romance From Another
Day'

→
**THE CHRIST STORY**

←
**THE MASSACRE OF
ST. BARTHOLOMEW**

→
**THE MOTHER AND
THE LAW**

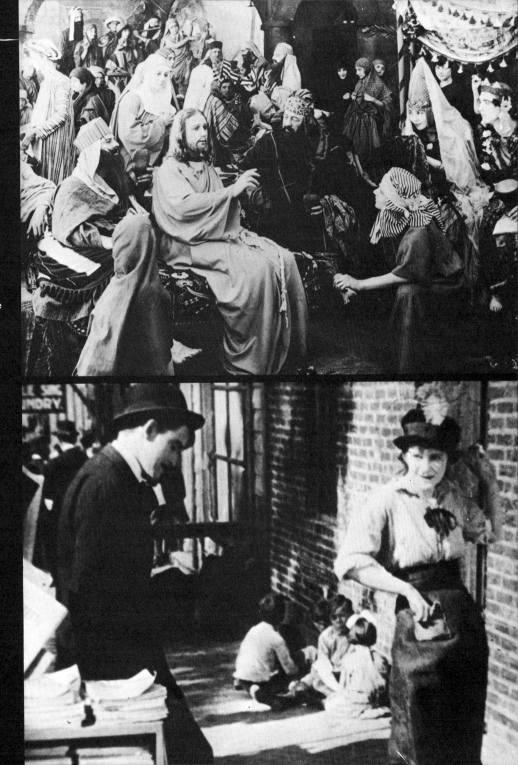

## The silent films of S. M. Eisenstein from particular anecdote to generalization

Out of Griffith's attainments and errors Eisenstein evolved the film of ideas, of persuasion

← **STRIKE**
1924

→ **THE BATTLESHIP POTEMKIN**
1925

← **OCTOBER**
1928

→ **QUE VIVA MEXICO!**
1932

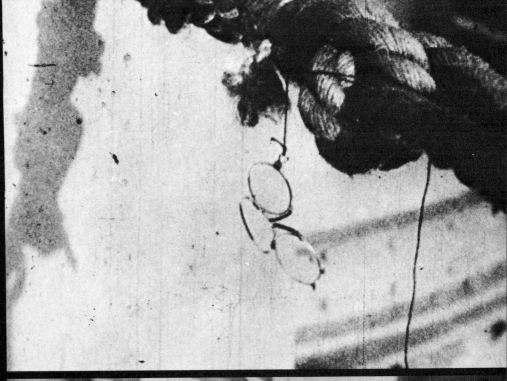

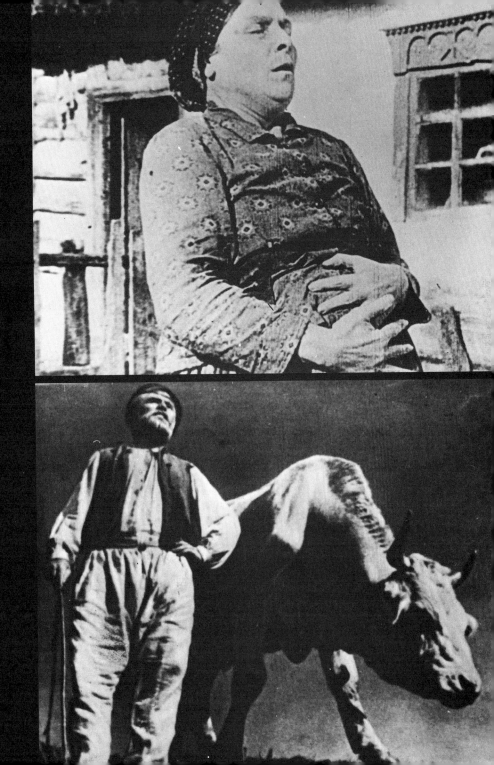

# The need to live: the acceptance of Communism

←
V. I. Pudovkin
MOTHER
1926
from the novel by
Maxim Gorky
Direct emotional appeal

→
A. P. Dovzhenko
EARTH
1930
Censored by the puritans
(not the politicians) in
1930. The cuts were
restored in 1958 revealing
the last silent masterpiece
of cinema

←
V. I. Pudovkin
THE END OF
ST. PETERSBURG
1927

→
EARTH

The need to live: the
acceptance of
Capitalism

Robert Wiene (Berlin)
THE CABINET OF
DR. CALIGARI
1919
designed by painters
Walter Rohrig and
Walter Reimann, and
architect Hermann
Warm
Script Carl Mayer

→
E. W. Murnau (Berlin)
SUNRISE
1927
designed by Rochus
Gliese
Script Carl Mayer

—
E. W. Murnau
THE LAST LAUGH
1924
Murnau directing Emil
Jannings
Designed by Herlth and
Rohrig
Script by Carl Mayer

→
SUNRISE

**The silent film was international**

René Clair
**AN ITALIAN STRAW HAT**
1927
In Paris, as in Berlin, there were no trade unions, no work permits for foreigners. Clair, the Frenchman, was working for white Russians; Dreyer, the Dane, for Frenchmen. Buñuel, the Spaniard, made his first tentative sound film for a French patron

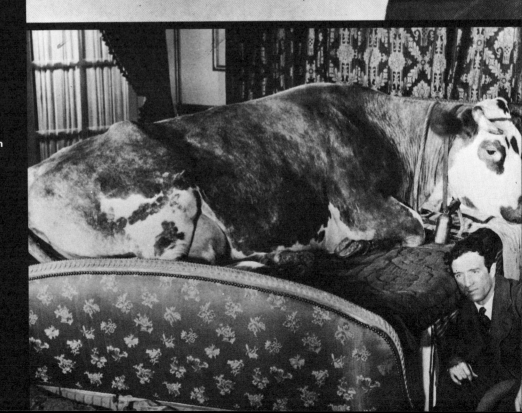

Carl Dreyer
**THE PASSION OF
JOAN OF ARC**
1928

**Early panchromatic
and late silent**

Luis Buñuel
**L'AGE D'OR**
1930
**The end of private
patronage with the
coming of the sound film**

**NANOOK OF THE NORTH**
1922
with orthochromatic
negative

**Robert Flaherty
from orthochromatic
to panchromatic
This man changed the
look of cinema**

**MOANA**
1926
with panchromatic
negative

# The Phase One period, to the end of the 1920s, had a humble birth in the remnant of

the pre-1914 paternalistic world. Referring back to Professor Huaco's 'the impact of political, social and economic variables on the exigencies of film production', the external pressures in the early days of film-making are clear; an industrial revolution, and a new population in need of some circuses with their bread. Some perceptive vaudeville artists looking for ideas with which to refurbish established theatrical acts seized on and adapted the mechanical inventions of the early industrial engineers, and created an easily portable form of entertainment. The new audience shackled by long hours and small wages were amused and entertained cheaply. Society, in which these activities occupied a small niche, was shattered by the First World War, during which the Russian Revolution thrust new social *mores* into the international scene. In the aftermath of the shocking slaughter of the war the populations of the Western world were exhausted. 'Politics' was left to the professionals (in particularly bad odour at this time in history), the majority of whom buried their heads in wish-fulfilment, hoping that threatening radical ideas, and new influences such as the rising trade unions, would evaporate if ignored. Empires, geographical and financial, were still thought by the affluent and privileged to be impregnable. But, against this class complacency, everywhere the *status quo* for the millions, which had recently suffered so many assaults on the assumption that the world could not be changed, was cracking. Thinking was confused, but ideas born out of disillusion slowly changed people. In cinema by 1929 the unsophisticated vaudeville artists, who had been the keystone of the early films, were dying out. The first mechanical processes for film-making had been superseded by new inventions, many of which stemmed from the necessities invented for use in the First World War (a sequence of events which was to be repeated after the Second World War). A few pioneer artists of many nationalities, using clumsy tools and materials with astonishing imagination, had begun to make experimental films for a small international audience of film addicts. Apart from the work of these miscreants, this form of entertainment was judged to be both vulgar and philistine suitable only for the riff-raff of the population. The mass audience wanted only a-political action films with heroes and stormy love stories with happy endings, housed in the architecturally garish cinemas, the 'temples of dreams'. The men of commerce wanted only money.

53

**Lewis Milestone**
1895–
Director and Editor

**Alfred Hitchcock**
1899–
(and Anny Ondra: *Blackmail*—
one face, another voice)

54

## Phase Two
## The Early Sound Film

There was no precedent for the coming of cinema, silent or sound. Formerly, if an artist found traditional materials insufficient he experimented with other existing substances. The devices of cinema were invented by engineers as a means of photographic record, they were exploited for commercial ends and caught the imagination of entertainers such as the conjuror Méliès, who had hitherto been content with the theatre and its repetitious performances.

Attitudes of film-makers to the introduction of sound were riddled with prejudice. Snobs of the silent film would have nothing to do with the talking picture, though the more subtle among them declared that some of their favourite films were talkies. The progressives tended to overdo their enthusiasm and just couldn't wait to have a go. It took years for the sound-track to be taken for granted and used and abused unselfconsciously.

The banal ways to apply sound to the silent film were either to make silent films with a sound-track of music and effects or to make film records of stage productions. For the latter they set up four cameras each loaded with ten minutes of film in clumsy sound-proof booths (from which the cameraman sometimes fell out after ten minutes in a dead faint). They dangled one microphone overhead. Later the film-editor intercut the four negatives anchored to the one sound-track. The sound-track was never cut at all, since it constituted one reel of film, nor at first could other sounds be added to it by re-recording.

The lighting cameraman had to compromise. He set up his lights serving all four cameras at once and sacrificing correct positions because he had to avoid the shadows cast by the microphone and the boom or rod from which it was hung. Film directors shared their function with dialogue directors. Films had to be made indoors, and exterior scenes involving dialogue had to be simulated in the stillness of the studio: the open air was too noisy even in the countryside.

Anchored to the constant speed of the sound-track, the speed of the picture camera could no longer be varied at the director's desire. And all the time those interlopers, sound engineers aiming at scientific accuracy, interfered with the temperamental atmosphere of film-making, vetoing voices of unusual character, insisting on flat clarity of speech and precise levels of volume of sound, unable to record a real shout or a real whisper, demanding compromises to meet the narrow limits of tolerance of their as yet primitive equipment. It was a hell of mediocrity until the non-conformists began to find a way.

The first improvement was to restore the use of the single camera with the scene lit and recorded from one single viewpoint. This brought the opportunity of perspective into the sound recording, since the microphone can be set closer when the single camera is brought near its objective. Then later cameras were made sound-proof and the awkward booths abolished.

But it was some time before real flexibility was achieved. At first the sound could only be carried on the one original track, usually recorded in synchronization with the picture. This meant that background noises, traffic passing, or bands playing had to be recorded at the same time: a sequence in a night-club with jazz bands, dancers, diners, and the rest demanded an exact joining up of the musical score in preference to all other considerations and in total disregard of the flow of the drama. Film-editors had to be able to read a musical score and under supervision to make imperceptible cuts in the music itself.

On one occasion, to remove a whole chorus from a piece of dance music which was recorded behind a series of dialogue scenes, I had to build a bar of music out of chords and musical phrases to produce a modulation from one key to another. Luckily there was no dialogue on these particular sections of sound-track. The dramatic action gained from being tightened up but may have faltered momentarily at the arbitrary manner in which the cuts were made.

Probably the most ambitious example of single-track film production is the Universal picture *All Quiet on the Western Front* (1930), outstanding among the wave of anti-war films and plays which began to appear a decade after the armistice of 1918. The director, Lewis Milestone, had been a leading film-editor and had evidently designed his sound-track as a positive element in his shooting script. There is a memorable tracking shot (at a time when few dared to shift the camera while shooting with sound), which begins in a street on a German military band leading volunteers to training. The camera tracks back through an open window, passing close to the militant schoolmaster haranguing his class and stops in a long-shot from the back of the classroom. The microphone, in those days unable to track, remains in the street, leaving the voice of the master unheard. To this day audiences accept this, though in a film nowadays there would be a trace of the master's voice competing with the din of the military band as the camera passes close to him. The next shot, close on the master, carries his voice over sounds from the street outside. The sound of the battle sequences is caught equally effectively.

The public eye had long been accustomed to the mounting of shot against shot for shock, but it took years for the public ear to reach this tolerance or anything like it. In a silent film one could watch people going about their business quietly at home, cut to a busy street, and once the point had been made, cut back to the quiet home. But what happened to the audience when the crude sound of noisy traffic broke into and out of the quiet sound of the house? Discomfort. So the conventional approach was to suggest the change of sound with music and the realistic approach was to stay in the house and make the point about the street in the dialogue at home. And think of the money you saved. A non-conformist could cut to the street and keep the dialogue in the house running at the same time, breaking it perhaps with some violent sound like the screech of brakes. But this was a notion that would only be accepted by the producer after practical demonstration. To put this into the script was asking for trouble.

The Germans were in the best position to profit by the adoption of sound. Their Tri-Ergon sound system had been patented in 1919 and had been incorporated into Tobis-Klangfilm, the leading system in Germany. The Tri-Ergon patents were later licensed to the American Western Electric system. Tobis got off to a head start once the time proved to be ripe. Moreover the German dominance in studio techniques, in design, building sets in perspective, simulation of outdoor scenes, trick work in and around the camera, gave them a confident lead in exploiting the limited resources of the sound-track to the full. When the National Socialist Party came to power during the depression of the 1930s, political and racial censorship throttled a thriving industry as had happened in Italy ten years before. It is a sad fact that while the fall of Mussolini ten years later awakened into renaissance the dormant tradition of Italian realism, the fall of Hitler in 1945 did nothing to revive the German cinema whose great asset, the mastery of formal design, was now outmoded, invalid, a thing of the past. The Germans who had been capable of the more human, less formal, approach which was now coming into fashion had fled the country long before and their influence had withered away.

But in the brief period from 1929 to 1933 the German attitude to the sound film was anything but conservative. In visuals they had the tradition of design and as for sound, music was in their blood. The silent film had had international appeal and a market limited only by the circumference of the world. Dialogue is specific, its import often local, and in translation demands such free and inspired interpretation into the colloquialism of another language, that the talking picture inevitably imprisoned itself within the frontiers of language. Hollywood became yet more of a sausage machine by casting each part in a film three or four times over and under one American with subservient foreign directors playing each scene in different languages with different casts in turn. Here were all the disadvantages and none of the advantages of using a computer. The results were mechanically approximate versions in French, Spanish, and German of an American film. Dubbing of voices came later after the introduction of re-recording.

The Germans gambled on the international appeal of their music. They reworked operettas and musical comedies into film continuity, recorded the music separately and played it back in the studio for the actors to match in mime. In these musical sequences the camera work could be as free and flexible as in a silent film. They invited foreign producers to remake the films in their own languages on the sets which they left standing in their huge studios. The music sold the films. Pre-recording of the songs in ideal conditions was no strain on the singers. When, on the contrary, Pabst made *Don Quixote* (1933) as a musical film[1] and Chaliapin refused to mime before the camera and out of purism sang over and over again until the shot was visually and orally acceptable, he destroyed his voice. Until his death four years later he never gave another satisfactory performance.

The Latin countries had developed no sound systems of their own. When Carl Dreyer designed his *Passion of Joan of Arc* as a sound film to be shot on panchromatic negative, his French backers in 1928 had to persuade him to make it silent as they could not afford to let him work in London, where the first French talking pictures were being made. The result looked superb, but only connoisseurs sought it out. Paris audiences demonstrated against the impact of American dialogue, and partly to win their goodwill Paramount set up its foreign version organization at Joinville, engaging distinguished, unemployed Europeans to remake Hollywood films with local stars. Nothing but discord and confusion ensued as individualists refused slavishly to copy alien entertainments.

Tobis meanwhile installed in Paris a rival organization and engaged René Clair and others to make original subjects in their own languages. The German approach, more modest and far more imaginative, was as successful in foreign markets as in France. Instead of talking pictures they made musical films which needed a minimum of titling to be understood abroad.

The Americans saved themselves from disaster and the rest of the world from utter frustration by introducing in 1932 the system of re-recording, or mixing, a number of different sound-tracks on to one master track which made it possible to synchronize into an orchestration of sound-tracks recordings of voices speaking in any language, so long as the dialogue when translated would appear to be synchronized with the original lip movements on the screen.

This invention killed the canned play, the filmed record of a stage production, as a necessary element in film entertainment. The sound-track no longer had to be regarded as a built-in obstacle to the flexibility of the medium.

Nowadays any number of tracks can be orchestrated against each other

[1] In two languages, French and English.

and re-recorded on to one master track or stereophonically on to as many as six tracks. In the early days channels for re-recording four tracks on to one master track made it possible to differentiate between sound close-up (usually dialogue), sound at a short distance (dialogue again), sound effects, and music. So accustomed was the world to hearing music with its films that its absence produced an unease. The use of the range of sound stretches from total unison with sight, that is to say providing in absolute synchronization the sound of what can be seen at the same time, to counterpoint which suggests a more remote relationship, comment or contrast, when laid against the moving image. Seemingly inappropriate sounds accompanying way-out visuals may introduce a new style, a new direction. No extremity can be discounted if it fulfils an imaginative necessity.

Total unison is an effective form of concentration and is capable of aiding recognition at speeds faster, I believe, than the brain can assimilate in life. In editing an American serial film with sound in unison, I found myself increasing the tempo towards one climax to the point where it was necessary to recognize in a close-up a spot of blood on the ball of a thumb caused by the prick of a poisoned dart, a matter of life and death naturally. In finally trimming down the action I reduced the close-up to five frames: at twenty-four to the second, this represented one-fifth of a second in which to establish a plot point, not just an effect of editorial fireworks. The blink of an eye takes longer than that. Image and sound in unison had led the audience to concentrate their attention and their concern on the thumb. I believe that if the film had been silent, the close-up would have had to be held longer because the brain would not be so attentive through the eye alone. An example of the opposite effect, the slowness of the brain to grasp an unexpected image, comes out in Resnais's *Hiroshima mon Amour* at the point where the first flashback to the German soldier at Nevers occurs. The image is of the dead soldier's hand in close-up. On seeing it for the first time, experts estimated the shot to be flashed on the screen for less than a second, say twenty frames, whereas on examination one finds the image is held for forty frames.

A more complex case is the bloodshed at the tragic climax of *The Next of Kin* (1942) which Winston Churchill asked to be toned down. On measuring the fragments removed, none of which lasted one full second, I found that nausea in the audience was caused by some thirty fragments each of a few frames, lasting barely twenty seconds in all.

Experiences like these throw light on the implications of censorship, of commercial interference with the length of completed films and of film prints reduced in length by wear and tear. The layman discounts such interference as trivial because he has no clue to the nature of the missing material. But to

**Humphrey Jennings**
1907–50
Britain's Vigo

the film-maker such a cut is an open wound or amputation. The layman judges film time from his experience of real time, yet the two have nothing in common even in the sound film with its fixed speed, as anyone can discover who tries to justify the capture of ninety minutes of continuous action on ninety minutes of film. Film time is organized, it is man-made.

The situation in those early days of cinema's second phase was complicated by the attitude of devotees of the silent film who refused to adjust themselves to the new order. Those who welcomed the challenge of sound regarded unison, or actual sound, as a utility, and were far more interested in the possibilities of commentative sound and of sound mounted in counterpoint to the visuals. They realized that a sound or group of sounds could constitute an aural image or shot, that the laying of sound image against visual image could form an orchestration far richer and deeper and more significant than the musical accompaniment to a silent film. I remember underlining the loneliness of a prisoner awaiting judgement in a cell with the whistle of a distant train echoing over a windy landscape, and the indecision of a man awaiting arrest with the urgent bell on a fire engine approaching and dropping a quarter tone in pitch as it passed and faded into the distance. Encouraged by the example of Alfred Hitchcock in his first sound film *Blackmail*

(1929),[1] René Clair in *Sous les toits de Paris* (1930), and Josef von Sternberg in *The Blue Angel* (1930), we began begging the script-writers to see and hear where formerly they had only seen, and not to limit vision by relying only on dialogue to tell their stories.

At first we were asking too much of the sound engineers and of their recording equipment. I mentioned earlier the inadequacy of the machinery. Microphones were insensitive and directional: their field of hearing was narrow. And the quality of sound recorded was liable to vary from track to track, so that when joined together they preserved no continuity of tone and volume.

Back in 1928 Eisenstein, Pudovkin, and Alexandrov had published a manifesto denouncing the obligatory synchronizing of actual sound and maintaining that sound should be mounted in counterpoint and as comment, thus extending to the sound film the principles of montage which they had practised in silent films. Now their proposals were becoming more feasible. Nevertheless while the literal recording of theatrical production on to film was no longer necessary, the influence of drama and the theatre persisted for many years and for many reasons. And uneasily woven into this hybrid were threads from the silent film entangled by conservatism and the inadequacies of equipment.

A short flash forward to the assets of cinema in the 1960s may enable the reader to sympathize with the handicaps of film-making thirty years before. Nowadays, eschewing the old-fashioned film studio, a small unit can shoot long continuous dialogue scenes with hand-held cameras operated from a bathchair or a baby carriage, minute microphones concealed in clothing, negative film scarcely needing any booster light, high quality sound recorded on magnetic tape, and with camera and sound recorder separate from each other but held in synchronization by radio or by accurate crystal control. Thirty years ago this was not a dream: to suggest such an idea would have lost you your job.

The Germans could achieve a passable imitation of this, either by elaborate and costly construction, too elaborate for the normally small sound stage, or by brilliant trickery with models built in perspective, sometimes reflected in mirrors, and by using dwarfs and children to represent distant adults. In 1932 the Americans introduced the back projection behind the actors in the studio of scenery shot on location which saved the cost of elaborate construction work and allowed the faking of dialogue scenes apparently staged out of doors. Back projection was originally devised to exaggerate the size of the

[1] In *Blackmail*, begun as a silent film, Anny Ondra, the Czech leading lady, spoke little English. Hitchcock's solution was to have an English actress, Joan Barry, speak the lines into a microphone out of shot while Anny Ondra mouthed the words before the camera.

animated models of prehistoric monsters in scenes involving live human actors: *The Lost World* (1932), *King Kong* (1933). But it all had to be attained by pre-planning months ahead with no allowance for improvisation which is the spark of life in most films. And splitting into short scenes was essential. At that time the backbone of cinema was the mounting of the separate pieces of film, the element which no other art possessed, the unique asset of the art of the moving image. Griffith had introduced it, Eisenstein had stretched the possibilities, Stroheim was scorned for his failure to understand its power.[1]

So while Stroheim forty years ahead of his time worked with orthochromatic deep focus in the genuine surroundings of his subject *Greed*, and thereby still manages to stagger a modern audience even with a silent and mutilated film, the rest of his generation of entertainers mistook artifice for art and fragmentation for flexibility. When sound came in, these physical drawbacks were accepted as the natural characteristics of an art form, the elements which brought an art into being. In fact they were primitive elements that needed to be superseded as early as possible. But they had to be suffered until the late 1950s. And they were suffered gladly by some people for many reasons.

Marxists had proved to the politicians that passive audiences can be led along a chosen line of argument by montage, by being shown only those elements of the scene that had been selected to carry the sponsor's message, exposing only what the sponsor wanted the audience to see. The television commercial owes everything to Eisenstein. The ambiguities of present-day cinema (the long flowing scene (in French *plan-séquence*) with action in foreground and background demanding equal attention) are anathema to the politician for they allow the viewer freedom to follow more than one thread of narrative or argument simultaneously on the screen.

The modern audience tends to agree to differ. But dividing an audience can lead to controversy, to unease, self-consciousness, and to loss of concentration; and this is bad for trade. Hence commerce lined up with the politician in endorsing fragmentation. The commercial producer took away the material directed by the artist and hired an editor to assemble the film in such a way as to appeal to the widest possible public. He differed from the politician by insisting that the content must be escapist, lacking all comment that might cause divisions in the audience.

When Stroheim edited his material in the camera so that it could be assembled in only one way, his own, commerce drove him out of circulation.

The critics, dazzled by the novelty of montage, endorsed the opinion of politics and commerce. And physically the loss of deep focus engendered by the adoption of panchromatic negative made it necessary to 'pull' or change

[1] Lewis Jacobs, *The Rise of the American Film* (New York, 1939), page 350.

focus with every movement of the camera or every shifting of the point of interest within the camera's field of view. This manoeuvring demanded skill in timing and execution and so added to the cost of production, already much higher than in the silent film. If it was badly executed, it broke the illusion by making the audience screen-conscious. Again fragmentation was the answer to the problem.

To be fair to the Eisenstein school, it must be made clear that there is a difference between the Marxist meaning of the term *montage* and the original French meaning of the word, which is here and now called *fragmentation*. *Montage*, by Eisenstein out of Griffith, has become an essential element in cinema, but it is no longer considered to be the principal element. And it is now executed in the camera as much as in the cutting-room. As mentioned earlier, it is a collision of scenes, an instantaneous change of shot or change within the shot producing a dramatic effect amounting at times to a shock. It also, as I have stated above, keeps the field of view under the control of the film-maker.

Fragmentation on the other hand while using the assets of montage also uses the cut from shot to shot for convenience. When an actor rises from a chair, it can be more convenient, easier, cheaper, to light him seated in one shot from which he rises, and then to light him standing (he begins by rising) in a second shot, so that the two shots can be cut together on his movement. A smooth cut often deceives the audience into seeing no cut at all. It is more honest to call the smooth cut a joint since the junction of two such shots is scarcely perceptible and rarely remembered. A cut in montage is a positive act, telling at the time and remembered afterwards. Most cuts in fragmentation are meant to be a deception.

The revival of influences from drama and theatre was a simpler matter, largely one of economics and convenience. It is useless for the artist in cinema to be impatient of the existence of commerce: the two have to live as neighbours. No artist could have had the opportunity to express himself on the screen if commerce had not found it profitable to pay for the physical development of the medium. And these costs had and have to be provided by the support of a sufficient public, large enough to justify the financing of changes and innovations in equipment. The sale of tickets depends on quantity as well as quality of product. The year of the change-over from silence to sound, 1929, was a year of tense and dedicated effort during which the decision had to be made by innumerable producers, distributors, and exhibitors to commit into production sufficient subjects to keep the theatres open once they had been converted to sound projection, itself a costly investment.

A stop-gap had to be found to fill the vacuum during which the conversion could be executed, the subjects found, trials made, and errors eliminated in adapting artists, craftsmen, and players to their new careers. The logical stop-gap was theatre, the simplest sounds were dialogue and music and, as mentioned before, the outdoor world was too noisy and all direct shooting of dialogue was driven indoors.

A film composed of dialogue sequences which differed little from scenes in a play was made in days rather than weeks by a theatre director and this took care of the essential need for quantity of product, since the four language versions, which had to be made to replace the one hitherto silent version, had also to be made on a schedule no longer than that of the silent film they were replacing and if possible at no greater cost. To win survival was more important than to temper the scorn of many an onlooker.

And with the investment of 300,000,000 dollars by the banks, which involved the loss of much independence, the cinema did at least survive to bridge the gap. The situation was made more precarious by the collapse of the New York stock markets in October 1929 which set off the great depression that led to the Second World War. It is safe to say that if in 1929 the decision to install sound reproduction had been delayed by eight months, audiences would have dwindled beyond recognition and cinema would not have survived commercially at that time, since the cost of the change-over could never have been committed. As it was, the cinema became the one cheap diversion to which the public could escape. And cheap it had to be. Money was scarce.

Therefore the convention grew and was accepted to construct the script in dialogue sequences and to shoot the film with the most economical fragmentation consonant with some measure of dramatic effect. The script was arranged in two columns, visuals on the left and dialogue on the right, and it was possible to get the point of the vast majority of scripts by reading the right-hand column and ignoring the left. Cinematic effects dependent on an unconventional use of visuals were left to a second unit to produce. In areas like Britain where the weather is often unpredictable, exterior work was usually scheduled separately and often left to a second unit to shoot along with the 'plates'[1] for back projection. The producer, who co-ordinated all this effort, was naturally dominant.

Hollywood became renowned for its professional skill in teamwork. It is likely that in that famous Western film *Stagecoach* (1939), attributed to John

[1] In the long-shots in which the principal players could not easily be recognized, doubles were used, actors duplicating the performance of the principals while the latter continued with close work in the studio.

Ford, he may never have left the studio during the shooting schedule. The exterior work is credited to a second unit of experts directed by Yakima Canutt, who later contributed the entire sequence of the chariot race to *Ben Hur* (1959), the first unit being directed by William Wyler. Ford and Wyler acted as their own producers but their share of the work of the second unit largely ceased with the end of pre-planning and started up again at the beginning of editing. The first unit was for the expression of character, thought, and emotion, the second for action. Even on the first unit the deployment of extras and the crowd scenes were often the work of the first assistant director. Naturally a big, spectacular film has to be organized like a military operation: the megaphone, early an object of derision to onlookers, has long given place to the loud-hailer, and at times to radio 'walkie-talkie'. Incidentally, a spectacular film based on historic events invariably costs several times as much to re-stage as the original event itself cost, *The Alamo*, for example, ten times as much.

Smoothness, calculated tempi, and a shapely build to climaxes, a beginning, a middle, and a satisfactory end, happy if possible, a nice balancing of characters almost but not quite out of stock, laughs sprinkled at intervals among the more serious moments, these were the constituents of diversion. If time was not to be consecutive, any juggling was signalled to the audience by a system of slow dissolves or of wipes, the wiping away of a scene leaving another in its place. The audience was never to be left for a moment in doubt as to the time or place of the event on the screen. Teasing the audience was a rare indulgence for jesters like Alfred Hitchcock. The Hollywood scriptwriters lured by talent scouts from all over the world were past masters at cheating the censor: the face value of action and dialogue were innocent, the implications were often wittily suggestive.

For the first two or three years of sound film, the shape of the image on the screen (the aspect ratio, in the jargon of film) was nearly square. The silent image covered the whole area of the celluloid between the sprocket holes in a ratio of three (height) by four (width). The presence of the sound-track narrowed the image to three by three-and-a-bit and proved a most unsatisfactory frame for composition. In 1932 Hollywood reverted to the aspect ratio of the silent film by masking the top and bottom of the image in the camera and using a new projection lens to enlarge the image on the screen. The innovation spread across the world in the wake of the introduction of the sound-track.

There is more than technical interest in these facts. The square image still further eliminated the pictorial environment of the characters in close shot and justified the need to widen the screen. But lighting, lenses, and negative emulsions were still not advanced enough to restore the depth of focus which was the main asset of orthochromatic film, now superseded by panchromatic. As we have mentioned earlier, the problem of deep focus in panchromatic film was not solved for general use until the middle 1950s and then formed part of the transition from the second to the third phase of cinema.

Events in the first years of Phase Two had as much bearing on the conditions of filming as on the state of mind of the audience. In the Soviet Union the beginning of the first Five-Year Plan in 1929 put an end to the artistic independence and experiment in Soviet cinema that had fertilized world cinema during the last years of the silent film. Self-expression, denounced as formalism, was condemned. The Plan demanded the pursuit of socialist realism, by which they meant the bare statement of useful subjects and which is a polite term for ruthless political censorship.

Eisenstein, Alexandrov, and Pudovkin had spent some time abroad as ambassadors of Soviet culture, Pudovkin in Berlin as an actor, Eisenstein and Alexandrov on abortive attempts at production for Paramount in Hollywood and then on shooting *Que Viva Mexico!* (1932) for Upton Sinclair in Mexico—an unfinished film. On their return Eisenstein was assigned to teaching at the Moscow film school VGIK, Alexandrov turned to musical comedy which made him a rouble millionaire, and Pudovkin lost his identity by toeing the party line. Eisenstein was never given access to his Mexican material until in 1939 it was too late for him to revive interest in mounting it: his ideas had inevitably moved on.

The first film that was fully approved in the new party line, *Chapayev* (1934), was a bitter disappointment to foreign audiences and in future each new Soviet film was prejudged as dull and predictable until it might manage to prove its innocence. Italian and German cinema were equally suspect of Fascist insincerity and obviousness. The national sources of palatable cinema in the 1930s shrank visibly.

In France the world economic depression led to a slump in the film industry and to militant trade unionism mobilized against the internationality of the personnel involved, which had recently been inflated by Nazi anti-semitism. The situation was aggravated by the failure of Paramount's foreign version organization at Joinville. Where could be the next port of call for the internationals ('born in a wagon-lit, living from express to espresso,' as Jean Renoir once put it)? The obvious destination was London.

In Britain during the seven years until the threat of German invasion in 1939, the internationals predominated. The quantity and in some degree the quality of film production rose until in 1936, 225 feature films were being made, the second highest national output in the world. In January 1937 the banks and insurance companies refused to advance further funds and a slump became unavoidable.

The film which had caught the imagination of the city of London was *The Private Life of Henry VIII* (1932) made by Alexander Korda, whose career had led him from Budapest to Vienna, Berlin, Hollywood, Joinville, and so to London. His London Film Productions attracted the finance to build, equip, and exploit the Denham Film Studios. Satellite groups from the European continent and America gathered round him, the bubble expanded too fast and burst. The excuse was doubt concerning the renewal of the quota law, planned in 1927 for a period of ten years. The new law brought improvements, and production revived next year on a more sober footing.

Quietly during the period of cosmopolitan glamour in commercial production another fugitive from Joinville, the Brazilian Alberto Cavalcanti, joined John Grierson's documentary group, now transferred to the General Post Office, and introduced the imaginative use of sound in factual and propaganda films. Working on a budget lower than the 'quota quickie's', the group set standards which were to prove a vital influence on national public relations during the coming war, when the Ministry of Information took it over and titled it the Crown Film Unit. Canada and Australia were also to set up national film boards out of its example. To Korda the film was an elegant diversion, to Grierson a weapon. A blending of both influences was to carry the British film through the war with some honour, though neither man was here to take an active part.

In Hollywood the mood of the depression was reflected by the gangster film, which came to rival the Western for lawlessness and sensation, and by a flood of comedies in which ordinary folk stood up to big business, which was inevitably shown as corrupt and selfish. Just as in Indian films with contemporary themes the villain of the piece habitually wore European dress and larded his conversation with ridiculous English phrases, so in Hollywood films the wealthy man was the menace, his wife callous, and only his children might show signs of latent sympathy. All these symptoms were folded into the conventions of the well-made film.

In France the same conventions applied, but here the film-maker was less the servant of the producer. The tradition of the *avant-garde* did not die, although after one or two attempts to continue, the individual patrons who had financed the silent *avant-garde* began to jib at the additional costs of sound. The swan songs of these private films were Jean Cocteau's *Le Sang d'un poète* (1930), Luis Buñuel's *L'Age d'or* (1930), and Jean Vigo's *Zéro de conduite* (1933). Vigo (born in 1905), son of an anarchist journalist of Spanish origin, was a total product of the ciné-club movement who refused to be touched by

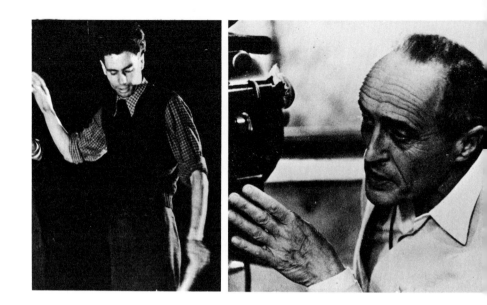

the conventions of commercial cinema. After organizing his own ciné-club and making two short films, he found a patron to finance his autobiographical satire *Zéro de conduite*, a poem distilled from the experiences of his unhappy childhood. Its sensational début in a Paris art house (Cinéma Artistic) in 1933 led to its being banned in France by Fascist influence until 1945. He died of tuberculosis in 1934 a week after the disastrous launching of his fourth film *L'Atalante*, a commercial project which he obstinately swung to his own style only for it to be mutilated into commercial shape as he lay dying. Fortunately for us a restored version still exists.

Vigo's whole output is frequently screened in one programme and represents more true values than the work of 99 per cent of film-makers. It was a revelation to the more discerning of his contemporaries and to those of the next generation.

René Clair dominated the French scene until he chose as his fifth film for Tobis *Le Dernier Milliardaire* (1934), a satire on dictatorship which the Germans naturally could not stomach. A French group backed the film, but it provoked angry demonstrations among Paris audiences with Fascist tendencies in an atmosphere which had been inflamed by the Stavisky and other scandals. Clair joined Korda in London and made no film in France during the next twelve years. Tobis replaced him with the Belgian Jacques Feyder, whose choice of subject, *La Kermesse héroïque* (1935), a skit on the placid

68

Flemish bourgeoisie under the Spanish occupation, was so much to their taste that, while the Belgian Rexists, a Fascist organization, rioted outside the theatre in Brussels, the Nazis in Germany took it to their hearts. Caring nothing about its political implications, the British found it devilish entertaining and handsome, as indeed it was at the time.

Clair's and Feyder's assistant, Marcel Carné, went on to team up with Jacques Prévert as writer and made a series of nostalgic, fatalist subjects, including *Quai des brumes* (1937), *Hôtel du Nord* (1938), and *Le jour se lève* (1939), which typified the mood of western Europe as it slid hopelessly towards the Second World War. The acceptance of the inevitable in their subject-matter was reflected in the acceptance of the prevailing formal, theatrical approach in their style. These films were exactly attuned to their time and they died with it. Now they are period pieces.

Among the other outstanding French film-makers, Marcel Pagnol and Sacha Guitry were unashamedly theatrical in their approach, Julien Duvivier followed the romantic, nostalgic line, Abel Gance clung to the traditions of the silent film, and Jean Renoir quietly and obstinately pursued his own bent which twenty years later proved to be the accepted way ahead.

While the last thing one can accuse Renoir of is rebellion, there was invariably an element of protest in his work, an inability to accept the hopelessness of the situation; there was vitality and exuberance in what he had to say and the informal way he said it. He learnt a great deal from Zola and from Stroheim, both sharp and unsentimental story-tellers. He rejected the formulae of well-made, well-balanced artifice, of theatre, of fragmentation. He believed that acting is the life of the film and he set out to encourage his cast above all to be comfortable. While his contemporaries tended to fit the action into the frame of a predetermined composition, he preferred to adjust the framing of his shots around the actors' exploratory movements in rehearsal. His reception among his contemporaries was like that of the one man who didn't dress for dinner. He is not a political person. Politics are not a preoccupation with him; they were thrust upon him. Yet he turned against the prevailing Fascism in western Europe, embraced the Popular Front and was an early name on Goebbels' black list of dangerous artists.

He let the daylight into his films: if he could not work wholly on location, he would insert views taken out of windows on location into scenes faithfully reproducing the building in the studio. He wanted his films to be lifelike and few of them have the balance of the well-made film which was the norm at that time.

While his contemporaries worked to make each of their films a little world of its own, in whose artifice the audience could take refuge for an hour or two,

Renoir in his films tried to show the audience an unfamiliar aspect of their own world. In so doing, he was evolving the embryo of the modern film, producing effects which were not appreciated at the time and are still valid today in spite of the inadequacy of the equipment at his disposal.

In his passion for linking the characters in his stories with their environment he anticipated the aim of the Hollywood cameraman Gregg Toland to restore the depth of focus which had perforce been abandoned when panchromatic displaced orthochromatic film. Toland was not ready with his new lamps and lenses and improved film stock until 1940 when Orson Welles came to Hollywood. Ahead of his time, Renoir had to do what he could with underdeveloped equipment. To emphasize the backgrounds of his action he had to renounce the close-up and the convention (in French, *champs contre-champs*) whereby conversations were habitually presented by shooting the speaker over the shoulder of the person he is addressing, back and forth like a game of tennis, since in these shots the small amount of background involved was usually out of focus. In place of this system, which had at least the asset of realism in the actors' stance, he contrived situations in which the speakers did not need logically to be facing each other so that their facial expressions could be studied for a longer period without a cut and in a wider field of view with the background in sharp focus. In fact he rejected the cult of fragmentation and followed the path of Stroheim.

Renoir was the first great non-conformist of the sound and panchromatic phase, the second phase of cinema.[1] In the silent film he quickly left the shelter of the *avant-garde*, but sound came before he had made a mark in commercial cinema and to find employment he had to make a concession to commerce before finding backing for the first sound film of his own choice *La Chienne* (1931), which proved too harsh and uncompromising for those days of depression. His first original subject *Toni* (1935), he wrote and directed with the friendly support of Marcel Pagnol, who furnished advice, studio, contract players, and distribution of the finished film. Here was a rudimentary stage of neo-realism, the reliving of a newspaper cutting about Italian migrant labour in the south of France. Pagnol by now had moved away from proscenium films to conversation pieces and to him too fragmentation was anathema: he liked to settle down and study a group of talkers without retarding the flow of conversation either for actor or audience by continually shifting the camera. But while Pagnol was to remain a listener, Renoir was more of a viewer: his groups came more and more to be an object lesson in the reflection of thought and emotion from face to face.

*Toni* was the beginning of his anti-Fascist period. With Jacques Prévert he made in 1935 *Le Crime de Monsieur Lange* (workers standing up to a dishonest employer) which was largely staged in a courtyard built solid on a studio lot with an eye to its cinematic possibilities. The action was more predetermined than improvised, as was also to be the case with the subsequent Carné-Prévert films.

Now Renoir began feeling his way in different directions like a runner taking to jumping, to weight-lifting. For the Communist Party he made a propaganda piece *La vie est à nous* (1936), lost during the war and rediscovered in 1969. In the mood of the Popular Front he tried to translate into his own style Maxim Gorky's play *The Lower Depths* (1936) and failed badly, proving that he was out of his element in alien places. For himself he made an enchanting diversion which he left unfinished, *Une partie de campagne* (1936) from Maupassant. On these last two films he gave employment to a young beginner Luchino Visconti, through whom he was to help to pave the way for Italian neo-realism.

And so to *La Grande Illusion* (1937), an original subject built out of the strength of his own experiences as a photographic reconnaissance pilot in the

[1] Early in 1928 in the silent film *The Little Match Seller* Renoir experimented with shooting interior scenes on panchromatic negative at a time when others were using it only for exteriors.

First World War and those of his friend Pinsard, who escaped seven times from German prison camps. Here was a protest against war banned in Fascist Germany, Italy, and Japan, and accepted with honour in every other country. This film justified Renoir's approach to cinema: the star of the film was an idea and the characters came and went as the subject required. Convention would have confined the action to the prison camps, but Renoir had more to say and followed the escaping prisoners to the frontier. Film-makers shook their heads at the intrusion of life into entertainment. The film abounds in group shots and one character is central only because the story demands his presence throughout: he does not dominate the action. The film, moreover, is compassionate and the only villain is war.

While *La Grande Illusion* was still in production, the French trade unionists in their thousands were buying through the Ciné-Club Liberté their seats eighteen months in advance for *La Marseillaise* (1938). Renoir gave his services and by cutting out the middle-man's, the distributor's, charges, the film-to-be was paid for at one sitting. But in spite of all the goodwill of the participants, Renoir's informal style did not sufficiently control this spectacle of popular nationalism. The film lacked urgency and the compassion it showed to both sides of the conflict was satisfying only to the few: it failed to penetrate far in subsequent general distribution.

Renoir had however already secured backing for his next two films, the first *La Bête humaine* (1938) from Zola, while for the second he floated his own co-operative on the lines of the original United Artists and became the sole promoter of *La Règle du jeu* (1939). Here was his own comment on his recent experiences and it exercised all his capacities and his talent. Like other rising artists, Renoir had been taken up by society and had absorbed acute impressions of the hollowness and decadence prevailing at the time. The rule of the game is the maintenance of appearances at all costs whatever is the truth behind the situation. The only genuine productive character in the story, an airman, is the one who suffers. The scene is a week-end at a country house with its upper crust of family and guests and its undertow of servants. The story weaves them together in a formal structure of intrigue. The style is simple but by no means casual. Behind the unassuming informality is a very sharp control. Renoir's job was made more difficult because he did not settle the casting until the last moment and he himself took over one of the leading parts, that of the onlooker who gets involved in spite of himself and has to be helped out. The story breaks the rule of the film game by involving on a more or less equal level enough characters to fill a novel or a play by Chekhov. When the job is done with skill, as for instance by Antonioni in *Le Amiche* (1955), which surely owes much to Renoir's example, the balletic flow of the action is itself a source of rare pleasure. In both cases it is an absorbing study to watch the characters being fed into the spectacle with no hint of indigestion.

The impact of the film in July 1939 on its first audience drawn from high society was horrifying. It was regarded as a cad's trick and some of the mockery in the 'director's touches', in the shooting party, in the burlesquing of a nationalist song, were regarded as blows beneath the belt. Nor did ordinary folk relish the behaviour of the servants. Ruthless re-editing could not save the film and on the outbreak of war it was banned by French censorship which has always been predominantly political.

Twenty years later both *La Grande Illusion* and *La Règle du jeu*, victims of Fascism, were reconstructed with loving care as closely as possible to Renoir's original intentions, which (unlike Eisenstein in the case of *Que Viva Mexico!*) he had not outgrown, and both films triumphed. Of what other films of the time can one claim as much, apart from some by Clair and Chaplin? *La Règle du jeu* is a clear example of what happens when two of the structural factors for success—current events and the capacity of the artist—are in advance of the third—adequacy of equipment—and hopelessly ahead of the fourth—the audience. This remark may seem trite to the spectator but can be useful to the potential film-maker.

Renoir's distress was submerged in the world events of that bewildering summer of 1939. It was bad enough to face the implications of an ideological war, but these were confused by the Nazi–Communist pact, which led to the banning in the Soviet Union of *Alexander Nevsky* (1938), Eisenstein's officially sponsored anti-Nazi film, and to the banning in France of the anti-Nazi *Professor Mamlock* (1938) because of its Soviet origin.[1] Then both of Renoir's masterpieces *La Grande Illusion* and *La Règle du jeu* were banned in France, the one for pacifism and the other for its demoralizing influence. Eisenstein was ordered to stage Wagner's opera *The Valkyrie* at the Bolshoi Theatre and to fraternize with Dr. Goebbels.

In an effort to detach Italy from the Rome–Berlin axis, the French sent cultural missions to Rome, and among them Jean Renoir, now a member of the army film organization, to set up a co-production.[2] Here he was welcomed by Visconti and his colleagues, Vittorio de Sica, Cesare Zavattini, Roberto Rossellini, Giuseppe de Santis, and others, many of whom disguised

[1] In Britain the opposite situation occurred. *Professor Mamlock* was banned in peacetime as a gesture of appeasement to the Nazi régime, and the ban was lifted on the declaration of war against Germany.

[2] Renoir found that Mussolini had impounded the Italian copy of *La Grande Illusion*, banned by the Fascist censorship, for his own entertainment and had himself suggested that Renoir should come to Italy to make a film.

their anti-Fascist inclinations in the ambience of the Centro Sperimentale di Cinematografia and its publishing activities whose patron was the young and naïve Vittorio Mussolini. Foreign films banned by the Fascist censorship were allowed to be screened privately as a means of research into new techniques. Renoir settled gratefully into this atmosphere, giving a course in film making at the C.S.C., showing his own films and sharing his ideas, including the notion which he gave to Visconti to make a film from James Cain's novel *The Postman Always Rings Twice*.

Italy entered the war and Renoir had to leave before his film of *La Tosca* (1940) got properly under way, but his influence took firm root and two years later Visconti's first and masterly film *Ossessione*, based on James Cain's novel, roused the fury of the Italian Government whose censors cut it to half its length. Realism, dormant for twenty years, was ready to replace Fascist artifice. It was like tearing aside a shiny false shirt-front and exposing the soiled linen beneath.

From the experience of *The Lower Depths* Renoir was acutely aware that he could only work satisfactorily in surroundings in which he had been steeped for years, his own climate and atmosphere from which he was now forced to uproot himself. With his beloved France under German occupation, he decided to accept the offer of an American passport and to assume at once American responsibilities. There are those who would have been honoured to help him plant his roots in Britain. Renoir found the American film capital very much preoccupied with its own problems in commerce and technique.

By 1939 Hollywood had managed to recover the world market which it had temporarily lost on the introduction of sound. By studying the varying responses of the different continents, the Americans were able to supply a richly contrasting range of programmes which would satisfy a wide spectrum of demands in each country. But as the markets shrank under the impact of war, this policy had also to be reduced. When the Germans occupied western Europe, the films that needed the western European market to recover their costs had already been withdrawn from production since this market had become nervous in anticipation. The general tendency was towards the more homely film. The outstanding victim of this withdrawal was Greta Garbo whose films, too serious to make a profit in America, had hitherto done well in Europe. Metro-Goldwyn-Mayer, her employer, persuaded her to appear in a comedy, Ernst Lubitsch's *Ninotchka*, but this too failed in the now restricted market. She made one more film *Two Faced Woman* and her contract was allowed to lapse. She has never made another film.

The designed film, which had begun with the German influence in the last of the big silent films *Sunrise*, reached its peak in the perennially successful *Gone*

*with the Wind*, completed in 1939 on the outbreak of war in Europe. The film was dominated by its producer, David O. Selznick, every camera position was designed on a storyboard and a succession of directors was restricted to the execution of a predetermined scheme. Rivalling *The Birth of a Nation*, this calculated entertainment based on a best-selling novel of the American Civil War and its aftermath in the southern states, has never ceased to attract mass audiences throughout the world. It served also to establish the Technicolour system in all except the iron curtain countries.

In this atmosphere the only stylish and influential American film of that period came to be made, to be seen and to be rejected by the mass audience. Orson Welles, born in 1915, formed the Mercury Theatre company in 1937, became the terrible child of American entertainment by the panic caused by his radio programme based on H. G. Wells's *War of the Worlds*, and was offered *carte blanche* by R.K.O. to make a film in Hollywood.

*Citizen Kane* (1941) became the most sensational first film of all time. It enabled the cameraman Gregg Toland to demonstrate all the research into lenses, lighting, and film stock that he had done between pictures to regain and surpass the assets of deep focus photography lost with the abandonment of orthochromatic film. Welles, adventurous man of the theatre and radio, proved to be the ideal co-demonstrator. When the available Hollywood stars refused to entrust themselves to his inexperience, the Mercury Theatre

## INNOVATORS IN FACT AND IN FICTION

*above*
**John Grierson**
1898–

*right*
**Orson Welles**
1915–

company admirably filled the breach with their discipline and their trust, for Welles was accustomed to cater to no man's comfort as Renoir would have done. The players in this first experiment had to be drilled to fit the composition to the square inch.

But there was more to the film than this, for his script, on which an expert screenwriter Herman J. Mankiewicz collaborated, for the first time pieced together the character of a dead man as a puzzle revealed by the five people who thought they knew him best. The film dislocated time in presenting facets of a man's existence in the manner of *The Quest for Corvo*, A. J. A. Symons's study of the writer, Baron Corvo, which may well have been Welles's model for the screenplay.

One may find in Eisenstein's *October* a parallel to *Citizen Kane*. Both films were highly self-conscious and by no means wholly achieved their aims, both were rejected by the crowd and both had a profound influence in developing the flexibility of the medium without ever being closely copied in their extreme methods. One look at *Citizen Kane* was enough to make Hollywood revert to the mixture as before. But film-scripts inevitably began to assume a new look and cameras new eyes to see with.

All this was as far from Elstree as is Elstree from Hanoi. In Britain on the outbreak of war the first abortive decision of the newly formed Ministry of Information was to close all cinemas for fear of panic during air raids and to divert the film workers to more useful employment. The internationals sought work in the U.S.A. along with a few British individualists, leaving the field open for a new generation of film-makers who were to receive generous guidance from the reconstituted films division at the Ministry. The argument there was, that while the propaganda film is invaluable, the skilful film of entertainment has the double advantage of diverting the native and impressing the foreigner as evidence of British morale. The films division was given control of all negative film which was made available to producers only after approval of each script. This veto, intelligently applied, raised the quality of the British product without removing the element of competition from the lack of which a nationalized output is liable to suffer.

The new film-makers, too numerous to mention here, were piloted by producer-impresarios, two of whom were outstanding, Michael Balcon of Ealing Studios, and Filippo del Giudice of Two Cities Films. Rationing of personnel and materials, all in desperately short supply, was mastered by remarkable organization. There was no time or opportunity for fancy work and that meant that reality had begun to creep in where studio work had prevailed before. There was an injection of realism which would have been termed 'neo' if it had ever been there before.

Every effort was made to simplify the issues involved in the war by declaring the conflict to be national, even racial so far as the Nazis were concerned, rather than ideological. In the summer of 1940 all projects for anti-Fascist propaganda were abandoned and the German and Italian nations as a whole were declared the enemy to be fought to a state of total surrender, an ambitious plan for Britain in a world peopled exclusively by enemies, defeated allies, and neutrals. From 1941, as the war spread, this policy was adopted by each nation which allied itself to us. In that year for example the Soviet Union was to name it the Great Patriotic War.

During the war, incidentally, Britain, cut off from most imports, many necessities, and all luxuries, used cinema to fill far more gaps than in peacetime. Annual attendances rose from around 1000 million in 1939 to a peak of 1600 million in 1946, whence they steadily dwindled to about one-third of that number in 1960 with cinemas closing in the same progression. Naturally Britain was one of the few European countries (and by far the most remunerative) to have access during the war to American films which flowed in as usual, though most of the profits had to be frozen during the emergency.

To the French the war was a matter of foreign invasion and occupation, first of the north and in 1943 of the whole country. The Germans imposed

their own films, which were boycotted by the resentful public, and their own censorship of French films, to which the brighter French film-makers skilfully adjusted their ideas. There was scant opportunity for the Nazis to convert an appreciable proportion of the French nation to their own ideology. Collaboration was almost invariably a matter of personal convenience rather than ideological conviction and sometimes was a cloak for hidden resistance.

Goebbels set up a company, by name Continental, to lead the French into the production of trivial entertainment, but it made no sense deliberately to make films that would repel audiences, nor has anyone ever found a means to compel people to watch repulsive entertainment against their will. Goebbels' policy was in fact so ill-judged that one of Continental's output of thirty films played to good houses at the Curzon and other British cinemas after the war. It was called *The Stranger in the House* (1942) from a story by Georges Simenon and in it Raimu as a lawyer delivered an eloquent speech in justification of National Socialism which the British critics and public accepted without a murmur. Another Continental production, *Le Corbeau* (1943), a 'whodunit' about a poison pen campaign, played at the Rialto Cinema in London to crowded houses after the war while its director in France, condemned for collaborating with the enemy, languished for over two years banned from earning his living.

A few important French stars were inveigled to Germany to make personal appearances, though some managed to obtain genuine certificates of exemption from doctors who had injected them with microbes of suitable diseases.

*far left*
**Michael Balcon**
1896–
Producer
(with Rita Tushingham)

*left*
**Laurence Olivier**
1907–
Actor and director

*below left*
**Filippo del Guidice** (on right)
1892–1962
Impresario

The sanest resisters worked in films which conveyed one point of view to the Germans and another to the French audience. For example, in *Les Visiteurs du soir* (1942), a medieval fantasy, when the Devil turns the lovers into stone, their hearts go on beating. And in this the Nazis saw and heard no harm. Its makers, Carné and Prévert, the only leading team which had remained in France, were allowed to follow this with another costume drama devoid of any political implications. *Les Enfants du paradis* (1944) served more than one useful purpose, deliberately giving employment for a long time to an enormous number of players and craftsmen who might otherwise have been drafted into war work. The film was timed for launching in celebration of the liberation of France in 1944 and its success everywhere helped culturally to revive prestige for the French nation much as did Laurence Olivier's *Henry V* (1944) to maintain British prestige in the closing stages of the war.

Weakened by their experiences, the French had little to celebrate and much to forget. Years were to pass before even one new personality in films was to emerge with the elements of greatness.

The Italian experience was different. Here the war was indisputably ideological. With the overthrow of Mussolini, the consequent German occupation and the movement of liberation from south to north, the realistic ideas of the liberals, whether Catholic or freethinking, and of the Communists burst forth in passionate expression with Nazism to take the brunt of the blame. There could be no more appropriately cinematic situation to exploit and the right wing of the nation had to lie low and take it. As the movement broadened to expose class injustice, a government swing to the right in the early 1950s brought capitalist pressure to bear to crush it. This movement, which the critic Umberto Barbaro labelled neo-realism, began naturally: the films were anecdotal and physical as silent films had been. When a house is burning, there is no time for research, for character study, only for action and reaction. Characterization is only incidental, as it reveals itself in action. Even if there had been no opposition from the right, the movement would have spent itself within ten years. Its participants grew out of its scope or relapsed into the clutches of conventional, romantic entertainment. But while it lasted, it held a blunt power that will remain a landmark in the development of the medium. Out of it grew the modern movement which along with the renaissance of the French film has taken the leadership in the third phase of cinema.

In assessing Italian neo-realism it is interesting to seek a parallel elsewhere. As in the case of Soviet silent realism, and here we refer back to Professor George Huaco, the Italian movement began at a time when the Government was too busy to exercise controls over cultural expression. In Italy in 1947 a government was formed of a coalition of centre parties. In 1949 the conventional majority of the film industry demanded government controls and aid to promote production, and Giulio Andreotti, head of the state department of 'spectacle', was put in charge. The Andreotti law included powers of censorship, political and otherwise, to discourage the making of films derogatory of Italian society. In 1946 women's suffrage had been introduced and the Church's influence gradually built up the female vote to outnumber the male so that in the election of 1953–4 a Christian Democrat government was elected, right of centre. By 1955 neo-realism was dead.

As long as the conflict in the films was anti-Nazi, the Italian people supported them, but the bourgeoisie increasingly resented any exposure of social injustice and particularly scenes derogatory of the Church. The films had to be made cheaply and even then got their costs back only in the export market, where social protest by foreigners is palatable since native income tax is not involved.

The importance of the new realism lies in its attitude, a new way of thinking which had evolved logically. The conventional theatricality of cinema lies in artificiality of plot, contrived design necessitating the use of studios, and dialogue demanding experienced actors who when they achieve stardom are marketed as personalities. In neo-realism the aim is behaviour, disarmingly natural, by unknown, unrecognizable persons in front of a camera that happens to be turning at the time.

In 1945 an anti-Fascist film-maker could count on only a minimal budget, was denied the use of an efficient studio, since most were housing displaced persons or were occupied by the armed forces, equipment was in poor condition, sound recording was cumbersome to use in natural surroundings. What was of paramount importance was the reproduction of actual experiences in authentic conditions regardless of technical perfection. It was a matter of extending the techniques of the newsreel to reproduce past events. At first they used actors in the parts demanding emotional range and non-actors elsewhere, working in a makeshift studio for the dialogue sequences and authentic surroundings for the rest. And they filled in the missing sound by post-synchronizing the voices of actors and the sounds of life into the edited film in a recording studio. Later they became confident enough to use non-actors throughout for the visual action and they used actors only for post-synchronizing the speech. They found they could work far more quickly in this way. And in fact in Italy they have done this ever since. Every performance became synthetic, the voice of one person harnessed to the face and body of another. It is the voice that betrays the amateur as opposed to the professional far more than the face. For this reason some films are more acceptable to foreign than to home audiences who resent the inadequacy of vocal intonation while the foreign audience is content to read the sub-titles or listen to a translation on the dubbed sound track.

This was a whole new way of making films that was thrust on a group of progressive film-makers as a result of social, political, and economic conditions that had become unendurable. The neo-realists made the best of a bad situation and because they had something vital to say and were determined to say it, turning their backs on convention, they introduced the art of improvisation and so found the element that has become the keystone of the third and current phase of cinema. They killed the formality of the theatrical film, they showed that art can exist without obvious artifice so long as the subject-matter is strong enough to hold the work together. A trivial subject cannot work in this kind of cinema.

The man who set the standard for the movement was a journalist, Cesare Zavattini, who has described its aim as the making of films 'utile à l'homme', of which an English translation might read 'films of value to humanity'. To him there is more in films than making money. He had started writing scripts before the fall of Fascism for Vittorio de Sica, a romantic actor who turned director when middle age threatened his appeal to the female audience. While Luchino Visconti, inspired by Jean Renoir, was making *Ossessione*, de Sica and Zavattini were already making *The Children are Watching Us* (1943), an indictment of the selfishness of parents, and Alessandro Blasetti, founder of the Centro Sperimentale, was shooting Zavattini's script *Four Steps in the Clouds* (1942), a touching comedy about country folk told in the realistic manner. All three films, utterly dissimilar, were signs that the sleeping beast was beginning to flex its limbs.

The first truly neo-realist statement was made by Roberto Rossellini, a young film-maker whose previous work for the Fascist establishment had shown that he was more interested in the medium than in the message. His film *Rome Open City* (1945) dramatized a tragic event in which communists and Catholics had jointly resisted the Nazi occupation. The film was begun clandestinely before the liberation of Rome in June 1944. Until now it had been customary to dream up an artificial, formal plot to set in front of even the most realistic background. Now someone examined the background and extracted from it the stuff which makes a drama. It has proved a dangerous, difficult formula, for the coincidences which create the frictions in life have to be accounted for. It is not enough to expostulate: 'But, I tell you, this happened!' The author has to force the audience to suspend disbelief, to accept the logic of the moment which in film is a moment, while in life it is a

moment arising out of the whole of time. Facts of life are often inexplicable, but they cannot easily be so on film.

The war bristled with anecdotes strong enough to inspire a number of such films. But the other two, and greater, neo-realists ignored the war and concentrated on social injustice. The Zavattini–de Sica team made *Shoeshine* in 1946 and in 1948 their masterpiece *The Bicycle Thieves*, while in the same year Luchino Visconti produced in Sicily his unique work *La Terra trema*, in which the subject and the absence of actors alone qualify the film as neo-realist. Only Eisenstein's work can rival the formal beauty of composition which Visconti brought to this deeply calculated film.

After his second neo-realist effort *Paisa* (1946), Rossellini abandoned the subject of contemporary Italy. Zavattini and de Sica went stubbornly on in the teeth of growing opposition, scraping together money from their own earnings and those of their associates to make *Miracle in Milan* (1950) in which only fantasy could provide a happy ending. Their last piece of un-diluted neo-realism *Umberto D* (1952) provoked an open rebuke and repudi-ation from the Italian Minister of the Interior.

Minor but honourable contributors to the neo-realist movement in political order from left to centre were Giuseppe de Santis (*Caccia tragica*, 1947, and *Riso amaro*, 1948), Aldo Vergano (*Il Sole Sorge anchora*, 1947), Alberto Lattuada

**NEO-REALISTS**

*far left*
**Vittorio de Sica**
1902–
Director

*left*
**Cesare Zavattini**
1902–
Writer

*right*
**Luchino Visconti**
1906–
Director

(*Senza Pieta*, 1948), Renato Castellani (*Sotte Il Sole di Roma*, 1947), Pietro Germi (*Il Cammino della speranza*, 1950), Luigi Zampa (*Vivere in pace*, 1947), Luciano Emmer (*Domenico d'agosto*, 1949).

Of the utmost importance in the third phase of cinema are the names of Michelangelo Antonioni, then a journalist, a maker of documentaries, and a script-writing assistant to de Santis, of Federico Fellini, then a script-writing assistant to Rossellini, and of Francesco Rosi, assistant director on *La Terra trema*.

In looking back over this remarkable movement in cinema, one has to discount the impurity of much of the music which covers so many of the films with a glutinous varnish of sentimentality. It is hard to understand how film-makers with a new, bold, and sharp approach could be so deaf to the banality of the musical scores which they allowed to be recorded into their work. Perhaps it was meant as a concession to the popular audience. If for instance the music could be filtered out of the sound track of *Umberto D*, this climactic film of the movement could never be decried for its sentimentality. And this flaw is particularly striking in a period when the foremost composers of Britain and the specialist composers of France were writing admirably for the medium.

The impact of the movement outside Italy was felt particularly in Asia,

America, and in France where cinema began a modest revival after the war until an outstanding personality emerged in 1950. Robert Bresson had made two films of a more conventional nature, *Les Anges du péché* in 1943 and *Les Dames du Bois de Boulogne* in 1944–5, both conceived theatrically and staged with actors in studios and on exteriors in the normal way. Then in 1950 a new Bresson emerged, stripped of the conventions he had previously accepted, presenting his version of Georges Bernanos' *Journal d'un curé de campagne* largely without actors, without studios, without theatrical dialogue, spare in the use of music which was entirely classical. He had learnt austerity from the bareness of Chaplin's style in comedy, contrast from the montage of Eisenstein, simplicity in the behaviour of non-actors and a general sense of the anti-theatrical from the works of Robert Flaherty and Vittorio de Sica. Of these the most immediate influence was the Italian. We all know how useless it is to challenge a Frenchman who refuses to compromise. Bresson is such a Frenchman. From now on he leaves out everything that is not essential: his films retain only those sparse elements without which they would fail to communicate. He never looks for a shot that is beautiful in itself: each image is neutral until it comes into relation with another. His avoidance of using anyone with the ability to act is carried to the extreme of imposing his own reading of the part into the bare voice and pure gaze of the participant. He has only himself to blame when things go wrong. And the only film in which this happened was *Pickpocket* (1959), the only one of which he was the sole author. Perhaps here he overtempted Providence.

The other four of his eight films are masterly: *Un condamné à mort s'est échappé* (1956), in which not one of the German guards is identified. *Le Procès de Jeanne d'Arc* (1963), *Au hasard Balthasar* (1965), the life span of a donkey, and *Mouchette* (1966) from Georges Bernanos' story of a fourteen-year-old peasant girl. Like Renoir before him, Bresson anticipated the third phase of cinema and in this phase he continues to hold his own. But since he makes no concessions one has to be in the mood to go out to meet him: he is never an entertainer. His clarity pierces and can hurt.

In Scandinavian and other small European countries the situation was different: a man could not live by film alone. The native market was too small and no formula yet existed to support production for the discriminating audience: that was to come later in the 1960s. Film-makers had to be versatile and if, like Carl Dreyer, they would not compromise over the choice of subjects for their long films they had to turn to the sponsored short film for their livelihood or share their productivity between film and theatre like Ingmar Bergman, Alf Sjoberg, and others. Their work naturally comes within the scale of the chamber films of the pre-Nazi German period and owes

84

little to the influences of the war other than an increased maturity. It gained international standing with the beginning of Phase Three.

In the U.S.A. meanwhile there were difficult times ahead which led physically to a situation resembling the one that provoked the introduction of sound. The first blow came when the allied armies forced the Germans back within their borders and the American department of psychological warfare flooded Europe with the backlog of Hollywood product for which the continent was imagined to be panting. Europeans had lived through cataclysmic times and the strain of occupation had been enormous. These stale films from the U.S.A., a country where not a single gun had been fired in combat, had a cold reception and absolutely none of the tonic effect which the psychologists had foretold.

The Americans found that they would have to tailor their merchandise to these scarred markets left to them after the iron curtain had descended. Stock characters manoeuvring in artificial surroundings were out: dramatic conflict would have to be enacted against the background of a world tempered by war.

In response to the success of the ridiculously inexpensive *Rome Open City*, Darryl F. Zanuck of Twentieth Century-Fox engaged Louis de Rochemont to produce in the neo-realist manner. He was a good choice, as anyone who studies his fortnightly *March of Time* series of news magazines (1935–42) can still recognize. But in the manner of the rich man clinging to his wealth with his eyes on heaven, Hollywood while stretching out one foot towards the new realism kept the other foot squarely set in the star system, and the compromise satisfied few. Nevertheless the tyrant studio began to lose its power: urban subjects began to be allowed the same freedom of location as the Western and the comic film had been given in the early days. And the financiers were to breathe again when they found that films with foreign subjects could be made more adequately and more cheaply wholly on location than in the studios of Hollywood, where salaries and costs were still geared to the scale of their markets before these had begun to dwindle.

The next problem was political. More than twice as many Americans had died before and during the subjugation of Germany, Italy, and Japan as during the First World War: ten times as many had been casualties. Hollywood had given a high percentage of its effort in support of the Soviet Union and against Germany. It was now to take a number of years for the creative talent to appreciate that our communist allies had withdrawn behind a curtain of mutual suspicion. There was an understandable bewilderment when it was realized that the recent conflict had all the time had ideological roots. The dilemma was typified in the struggle to define 'unAmerican activities' as communist and in the use of Fascist methods to overcome these activities. The talent of Hollywood, much of it already tested in active warfare, was bitterly tried to the point where the price of physical freedom was the betrayal of confidence.

Between 1947 and 1950 the UnAmerican Activities Committee sent ten Hollywood writers and directors to prison for refusing to betray themselves and their friends, and caused hundreds of others to be black-listed, mostly people who in Europe were regarded as liberals. Up against an unbalanced world market Hollywood began to suffer from imbalance of intelligence, which was intensified by the witch hunts instigated from 1953 by the Senate permanent investigation committee under Senator McCarthy. The persecution continued long after his fall from power in December 1954.

The American film suffered particularly because the pursuit of entertainment ceased to be voluntary and positive and became instead a compulsory avoidance of any political or social point of view, a negative occupation.

There is all the difference in the world between voluntary support of a total war effort and compulsory submission to a totalitarian effort in peacetime. For years the purveyors of ideas in Hollywood tasted the bitter flavours of an implicit police state. Some emerged strengthened but many succumbed.

The third blow to the power of Hollywood was the impact of the motor car and of television. That of the motor car was solved in the warmer weather by the invention of the drive-in cinema which set huge, unearthly silver moving images dangling under the night sky, silent since the sound came by small individual amplifiers through the windows of each car. But television cut the American audience by forty per cent between 1946 and 1950. The film distributors examined their foreign markets which were not yet affected by this intrusion; they considered raising the price of seats in the American market and above all the possibility of some counter attraction to the small, insistent tele-image that in America was free of charge once the receiving set had been installed. Their conclusion was a larger, wider cinema image in colour and with a depth of focus that could offer spectacle worthy of more than one viewing. This was the gimmick to divert the public from the cosy immediacy of their little television screens.

An example of the ...rtoon work of ... M. Eisenstein for ...s last film *Ivan the ...rrible* (1948). ...senstein used his ...rly talent as a ...rtoonist in ...esigning the ...mpositions, the ...oryboard, for his ...ms

# Characterization begins to emerge in the sound film

Lewis Milestone
**ALL QUIET ON THE WESTERN FRONT**
1930

Alexander Korda
**THE PRIVATE LIFE OF HENRY VIII**
1932

Joseph von Sternberg
**THE BLUE ANGEL**
1930
with Marlene Dietrich

Jean Vigo
**L'ATALANTE**
1934

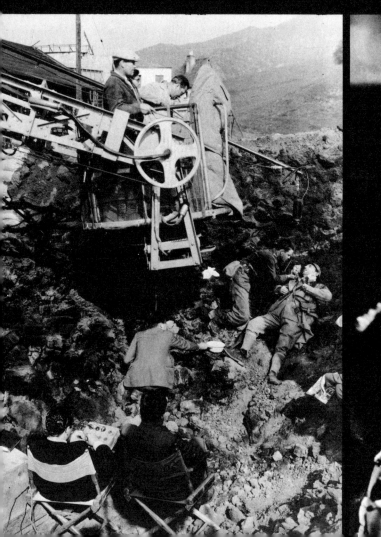

**Renoir in the Thirti**
from Griffith to Stroheim,
to Renoir and on through
neo-realism, the path to t
modern sound film can be
traced

←
**BOUDU SAUVÉ DES
EAUX**
1932
→
**LA GRANDE ILLUSIC**
1937
←
**UNE PARTIE DE
CAMPAGNE**
1936
→
**LA RÈGLE DU JEU**
1939

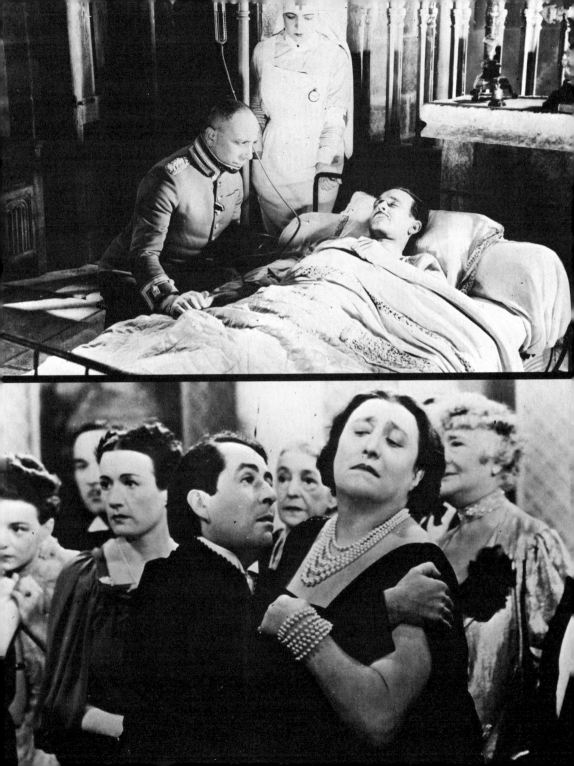

## The German presen
in French cinema

Not content to lease their
sound system in the
American manner, the
German Tobis concern ear
established studios and
production in France and
paved the way for their
operations during their
subsequent occupation of
the country

←

**René Clair**
**SOUS LES TOITS DE**
**PARIS**
1930

←

**Jacques Feyder**
**LA KERMESSE**
**HÉROÏQUE**
1935

Marcel Carné
LES VISITEURS DU
SOIR
1942
(above) Carné directing
(right) The beating hearts in
the stone statues

Marcel Carné
LES ENFANTS DU
PARADIS
1944
with Jean-Louis Barrault

John Ford
**THE GRAPES OF
WRATH**
1940

**Gregg Toland's
photography serves
both old-established
and newcomer**

Orson Welles
**CITIZEN KANE**
1941
**The most influential first
film ever made, and the
most rewarding financial
failure. Danger: Artist at
work in isolation**

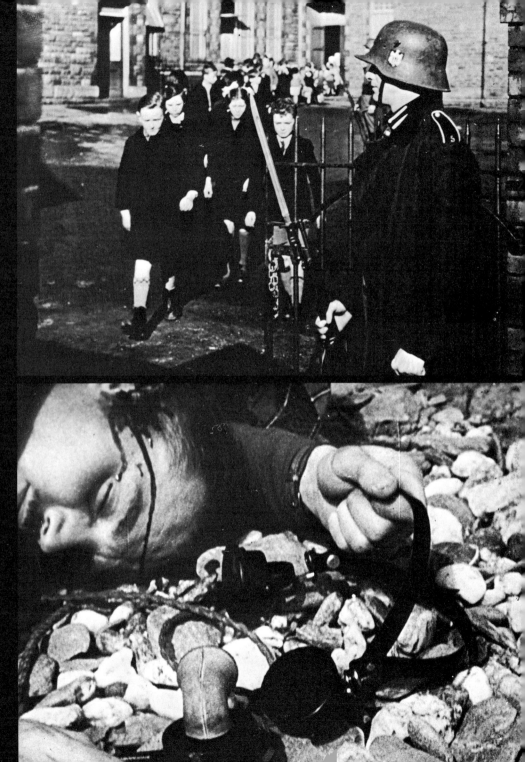

umphrey Jennings
**HE SILENT VILLAGE**
43
dice: the children lined
for deportation from
e village which was
urdered

he Second World
Var which
nmolated millions
hether in or out of
niform

norold Dickinson
**HE NEXT OF KIN**
42

S. M. Eisenstein
**ALEXANDER NEVSKY**
1938

Laurence Olivier
**HENRY V**
1944

Luchino Visconti
**OSSESSIONE**
1942
Anti-fascist, and cut by
50 per cent by Mussolini's
censors, the whole film
was revived privately
after the war

**Early Neo-Realism in
wartime**

Roberto Rossellini
**ROME OPEN CITY**
1945
Neo-Realism was palat-
able in Italy when the
villains were foreigners

The peak of Italian
Neo-Realism

Luchino Visconti
**LA TERRA TREMA**
1948
Set in Sicily (to the
Italians as Eire is to the
English), this was the
most stylish, uncom-
promising, and foreign
of Italian neo-realist
films

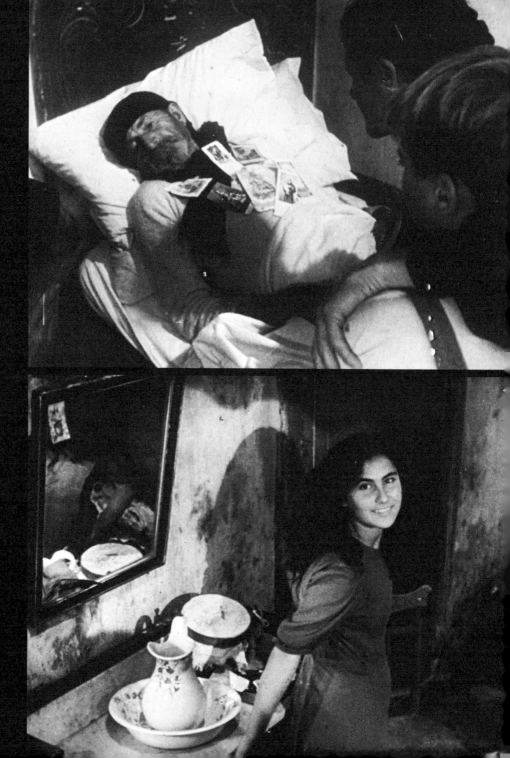

# Neo-Realism
# post-War

Rejected in Italy when the
villains were themselves
Italian

Vittorio de Sica
MIRACLE IN MILAN
1950

UMBERTO D
1952
This film, critical of the
social services, was
judged derogatory to the
Italian nation by the
Minister of the Interior in
an Open Letter to de
Sica

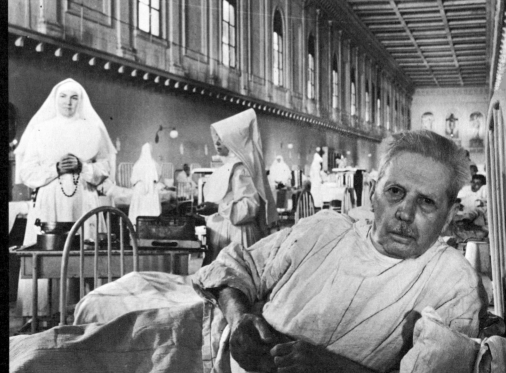

Akira Kurosawa
**THE SEVEN SAMURAI**
1954

**The Eastern and the
Western**

John Sturgess
**THE MAGNIFICENT
SEVEN**
1960

**The two photographic styles of Gabriel Fugueroa**

Pursuit of the stage
coach, from John Ford's
**STAGECOACH**
1939

**Salute to the Second
Unit: Yakima Canutt,
director**

The chariot race, from
William Wyler's
**BEN HUR**
1959

**At the time of the** slow change-over from Phase Two to Phase Three our four structural factors were decidedly out of equilibrium, as they had been at the end of the silent period. The historical background to the first ten years of Phase Two was the disastrous time of the Great Depression which spread across the world and not only affected the basic needs of life for millions but was also a spiritual devaluation. The frustrating blight of unemployment for able-bodied people with able minds unable to exercise even ordinary talents proved a traumatic experience. The times inspired a few visionaries to distil on to film their day-to-day existence. Some of the work was sombre, some counterpointed with gaiety, often a little frantic. They persisted through the accumulating apathy of the thirties. At the same time the hordes of refugees from the Nazi régime spread over the world; and parallel there was the Spanish Civil War, dress rehearsal for the greater war to come. At each point of the compass one saw the set face of the old ways of thinking which allowed nation after nation to slide into the Second World War.

Against this tapestry creative film talent, now embroiled in war, applied its imagination to record ideas of national urgency. From the advances in engineering and electronics, vital to the war effort, film-makers were acquiring tools far in advance of anything with which they had been able to work before. And their audience? By 1946 civilian life other than in America had been worn down to a shabby, frayed uniformity at best, and over much of the old world it had literally been razed to the ground. There was a huge audience looking for escape from worn-out homes and lives rationed in all essentials and deprived of luxuries.

The American film industry with the widest system of distribution in the world, worked on the basis of recouping their costs in the home market and making their profits abroad. During the war much of their foreign market was denied them. When they recovered this ground, they found an audience alienated by enemy occupation. The public was no longer satisfied with escapist *kitsch* on the shabby screens of out-dated theatres. The commercial complacency of the later thirties and of wartime evaporated in the post-war years. In America and Britain television became an established element in domestic life. In the world at large improving prosperity offered a wider variety of leisure occupations. There was choice: no compulsion to accept *faits accomplis* shown in buildings which are monuments to discomfort. Commerce wanted to go on making money, of course, but its gold mine, the make-believe image of the past twenty years, reeling across the screens of the world, was worked out.

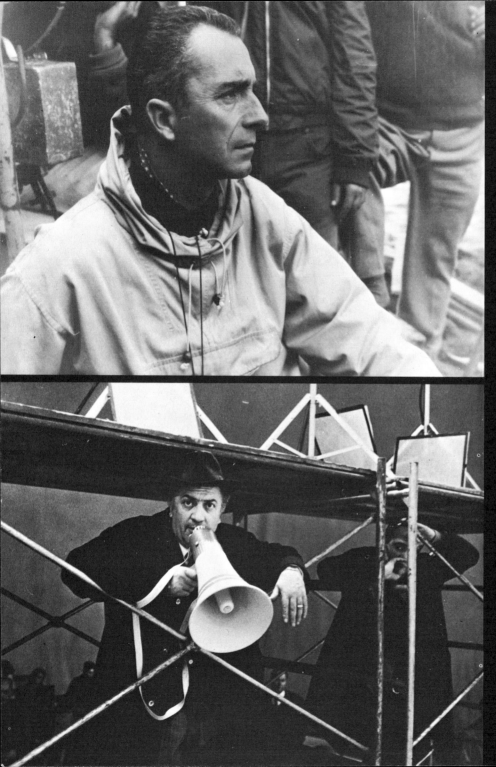

**Michelangelo Antonioni**
1912–
Italy

**Federico Fellini**
1920–
Italy

# Phase Three
# The
# Modern Sound Film

We can assess the first two phases of cinema, each lasting some thirty years, using hindsight to reconsider a personal, day-to-day experience. But Phase Three is a different problem, since it only began to have an effect physically some fifteen years ago and mentally even more recently, and it is still in full evolution. The tools available to date are here for all to see. But the mind and emotions, and indeed the economics, of film-makers are adjusting to the new physical possibilities of the medium from film to film in a manner that is fascinating to watch as a full-time occupation, but is liable to be bewildering to the layman and beyond any valid assessment.

This study, then, can only retire with as much grace as the situation allows, hopefully encouraging readers to continue their own discovery of cinema, an activity which demands more of the individual than has been apparent in the past.

The transition to the third phase of cinema, as occurred in the change from Phase One to Phase Two, was primarily pressured into being by the commercial men; the demands of their banks impelled them to find and develop new ideas which would make money. Audiences were becoming more experienced, younger marriages meant that family life was beginning earlier and was being entertained at home by television. Cinema-going was ceasing to be a periodical habit and people were now choosing their programmes by press report and 'word of mouth' reaction.

But the change-over from Phase Two to Phase Three has spread over a much longer period than the change from silent to sound film. The physical change was commercial and American, the mental change was creative and Latin. Let us take the physical first.

Showmen have always favoured a large screen but technicians have preferred a smaller surface, disliking the unpleasant effects of 'graininess' that blur the over-enlarged image. Technicians also recognized the difficulty of achieving an adequate depth of focus since the introduction of panchromatic negative film.

These were the main reasons why the traditional aspect ratio of three by four ($1\cdot33:1$) was universally accepted as the suitable proportion for the cinema screen, particularly as the back seats under the balcony of most cinemas could not afford a view of the top of any taller screen of adequate width.

A bigger screen could only be wider, as Paramount discovered in 1926 when to emphasize the stampede of elephants in Cooper and Schoedsack's Asian travelogue *Chang*, they enlarged the image to double its height and width by the use of Magnascope lenses, and found the film could only be shown in theatres without a balcony or by roping off the back seats where a

## THREE SUPERB CRAFTSMEN

**Henri Chrétien**
1879–1956

**Gregg Toland**
1904–48

balcony cut off the view. And the grain in the emulsion, quadrupled in size, danced biliously on the huge screen.

To minimize the grain 65 mm. and 70 mm. negatives were introduced at various times, particularly in 1900 and 1929, but the installation of projection proved too costly except in the bigger cities, as has happened more recently in the case of Cinerama. There was even in New York in 1929 a showman's stunt in which during the interval a projector in the ceiling threw the picture of an orchestra playing on to a horizontal screen which exactly covered the orchestra pit.

In its efforts to make the film more blatantly lifelike, commerce attempted to introduce to the public the three-dimensional image. But the only system immediately available was one which required the spectator to wear a pair of polaroid spectacles, a temptation to pilfer which proved very costly. Moreover no cameras had been constructed with the two lenses set as close together as the human eyes. Instead two normal cameras were set side by side in synchronization, but obviously with the lenses further apart than the eyes of an elephant. The result was a monster's eye view of the world, which reduced the scale of reality to that of an elaborate model. Buildings and vehicles looked like toys and humans resembled midgets. A two-dimensional picture taken from a roller-coaster on the move was far more convincing than a midget lion in 3-D, however three-dimensional its roar, leaping like a kitten towards one's lap.

The practical solution of the need for a wider image in the ordinary cinema was found by a French optician, Henri Chrétien, who in the First World War had designed a wide angle lens with a field of view of 180° for use in periscopes on the newly invented tanks. This anamorphic lens (which he called Hypergonar) was used for aerial still photography in map-making after the war and then adapted for motion pictures, squeezing a wide field of vision on to the normal 35 mm. negative. The process was reversed in projection.

In 1928 Claude Autant-Lara, a former art director, used Chrétien's anamorphic lens to make a silent film *Construire un feu* from a story of the snowbound north by Jack London, in which alternate reels threw wide and tall pictures on to the white-washed back wall of a Paris cinema with no balcony. Sometimes there were two or even three images side by side, as Abel Gance had shown the year before, using three linked cameras (and three projectors) in his huge film *Napoléon*, a process which he called Polyvision.

The idea of the triple camera cum projector was later developed as Cinerama, but it was bound to be superseded in favour of the less complicated image thrown by the single projector that can now be equipped for 35 mm. and 70 mm. film.

**Yakima Canutt**
1895–

Chrétien's system lay dormant until panchromatic negative and electric studio lighting could be improved to cope with a depth of focus from the close object to infinity. As soon as this was nearly attainable later in 1952, Twentieth Century-Fox Films bought the rights to the process, dubbing it CinemaScope, and gambled on improving the lenses and on providing spectacle to fill the new, wider aspect ratio of 2·55:1, which is approximately twice the width of the traditional screen.[1] In the traditional aspect ratio one, two, or at the most three, people filled the foreground of the screen and compensated for the lack of focus in the background. But with the wider area close shot and long shot could be present at the same time. Hence depth of focus was essential.

The influence of this system was so great that those cinema exhibitors who could not afford to install it masked the top and bottom of their screens to achieve a poor man's version with traditional lenses, and film-makers in country after country followed suit. Some used the ratio of 1·65:1, some 1·75:1 and those who played for safety adopted the ratio of 1·85:1. In the late 1960s this confusion of ratios had still not been resolved. Films are still being made in the traditional ratio in countries behind the iron curtain since they lack the currency to buy goods in the west and their own camera lenses have not yet been developed to achieve an adequate depth of focus. This is also true of their anamorphic lenses: in the CinemaScope-type films of Poland and elsewhere the focus is constantly being changed within the shot as the dominant characters move forward and backward on the screen.[2]

When a film composed in the traditional ratio of 1·35:1 (and a new film in this ratio nowadays is bound to be foreign to the English-speaking world and so almost certain to be sub-titled) is shown on a screen with a new aspect ratio of inadequate height, the sub-titles are shown and the top of the image is sacrificed. Heads are often cut off down to the chin and fine composition in mid and long shots mutilated. The sooner this barbarity is recognized as a breach of contract, the better it will be for the art of the film. The solution is to equip the projectors with sufficient lenses and masking plates and to remove the black border which conventionally frames the picture screen or to make the border adjustable electrically. Until this is done, the so-called up-to-date cinema will continue to charge full prices for showing less than two-thirds of any 1·35:1 film.

American producers in a further bid to provide a yet more powerful counter-attraction to television (at that time largely black and white and

[1] In anamorphic cinematography Panavision lenses have now superseded CinemaScope, though the latter are still used in film projection.
[2] Andrzej Munk's unfinished film *Passenger* (1963) is an example.

able only to transmit one sound track) insisted on using colour with Cinema-Scope, and finally added six-track stereophonic sound. The sound came at the audience from all round the building, which the producers believed aided the illusion of a third dimension when combined with the contribution of the anamorphic lens. In projecting the traditional aspect ratio the sound comes from behind the centre of the screen. The engineers were concerned that if the obvious source of sound was from the centre of the screen, and characters in the film were speaking while standing at each side of this enormous screen the effect would not only be unnatural but disturbing—therefore, every cinema would have to be wired to convey stereophonic sound to the audience —common sense and the economics of carrying out such a programme finally prevailed. One sound track served the normal cinema theatre and black and white photography was able to hold its own against colour.

Serious film-makers have been reluctant to use colour until their choice of subjects challenges them to do so. Their avoidance has been instinctive as much as reasoned. Superficially speaking colour is a step towards reality and certainly its judicious use is essential if you want to study surfaces. It adds a necessary dimension in factual films about people, places, and processes. But this dimension exerts such a magnetic attraction for a spectator that critical perception of meanings can be seriously impaired.

As in the case of music, colour should be an essential ingredient in the drama for it to be stimulating: as in *Il Deserto rosso* (1964). You could not appreciate *The Red Desert* on black and white television for instance. Colour is an asset to the *movie* but it can be a liability in the *film*.

Continuing the inventory of change we have to take stock of cannibalism. The drawbacks of television are mainly two, a threatening dearth of quality and the instantaneous impact which allows the spectator little foreknowledge to aid his choice of programme. One answer lay in transmitting known films on whose reputation the spectator could rely. But when the backlog of cinema films is exhausted, how can the lords of television maintain their ascendancy? By making new films which must gain a reputation in cinemas before being televised. And this constitutes the most dangerous threat from television to cinema. The wider image now used in the cinema cannot be transmitted in its entirety at one moment on to the television tube; the borders of the picture composition on all four sides of the frame are cut. If commerce decides to adopt a compromise aspect ratio which fits the television tube, this will mean reverting to the narrower image of the early film screen, a cinematically retrograde decision.[1]

[1] Cannibalism is already adopting new recipes. The fate recently accorded to a successful film opens up a filmscape of nightmare fantasy. Written by Edna O'Brien, directed by Peter

The new opportunity to compose within a wider frame sharply divided conservatives from progressives. Critics among the former sneered at the letter-box screen, as they called it, as suitable only for bedroom scenes, and they protested seriously at a retrograde step that would thrust cinema back into the theatricality from which it was trying to escape. Conservative film-makers found it almost impossible to learn to compose for a wide screen without laborious effort. Years were to pass before the ordinary spectator could enjoy a film without being made forcibly aware of the shape of the image.

Those who mistook the Scope screen for a two-dimensional proscenium opening and feared yet another return to canned theatre were the same critics who mistook fragmentation for montage and were steeped in the heresy that the main difference between theatre and cinema lies in the fragmentation of the image. These people had never proceeded beyond the primitive concept of the film as a photographic record, had never considered interpretation as more than the shifting of the camera. Back in 1953 the late André Bazin drew attention[1] to what one may describe as the *conviction* shot, the shot that is necessary to maintain the spectator's belief; for example the shot in *Where No Vultures Fly* (1951), in which Harry Watt included the lioness in the background, the child carrying the lion cub in the middle ground and the agonized parents in the foreground. According to heresy such a shot is not strictly necessary, being more theatrical than cinematic. On the contrary it is obligatory and the spectator rightly feels cheated when for lack of application, fear of danger, or contempt for the audience such a shot is left out by the director. Here, says Bazin, montage is forbidden. The whole scene should be played in one all embracing shot, long, mid, and close at once, however difficult it may be to organize.

Now at last with the physical assets of a wider field of view and a return to Lumière's depth of focus, the sound film was indeed coming into its own. Fragmentation of the image was no longer justified except in the eyes of commerce, and the deceptive, imperceptible joint of shot to shot had become a concession to inadequacy rather than an accepted convenience. The true

Hall and financed by an American distributor, *Three into Two Won't Go* was ranked among the Top Twenty films in Britain in 1969 so far as revenue was concerned. Bearing the same title as the original film, it has since been made acceptable to American television not only by being severely cut but also by the interspersing, throughout its length, of twenty minutes of new scenes written, directed, and acted by people who had no part in the original film. To quote Peter Hall (*The Times*, London, 27 Oct. 1970): 'It had the same stars but a totally different story. I know because I directed the original' and 'The new film is so predictable that it will only provoke laughter among the people who cared for the original.'

[1] André Bazin (tr. H. Gray), *What is Cinema?* (California, 1967), p. 49.

challenge of cinema began to be evident to serious critics and to the younger film-makers. And the nature of this challenge has no relation to theatre. Selection, emphasis, and timing in the silent film were largely controlled in the editing process in the cutting room. Now they had become an asset of the shooting process as well. This is what Renoir had been working towards during the 1930s with the limited equipment at his call: to show action (including speech) and reaction at one and the same time in the same set-up and to make the cut a perceptible, positive act. This was the end of the use of cinema as a photographic record of something going on. Cinema had become something on its own, transforming the physical action from the uncompounded to the compound.

This was the end of the bifurcation which derived from D. W. Griffith, the re-uniting of the two streams, on the one hand of *montage* initiated by Eisenstein, and on the other hand of the *plan-séquence*, the shot, longer in time, initiated by Stroheim, within which selection, timing, and emphasis are pre-arranged and fixed at the time of shooting and cannot be altered later in the cutting-room. Stroheim had sacrificed his career in defence of this principle. Griffith had made the director the dominant, controlling element in cinema. On Griffith's financial failure the producer superseded the director, who was forced to take his place as the leading element in the team under the producer. Now the director who met the challenge of Phase Three again became the dominant personality, the film-maker. And this he did by combining the assets already at his command, *plan-séquence* with its avoidance of fragmentation, and montage which makes a dramatic point of every cut.

To give a simple example, in *Ride Lonesome* (1959), a Western in Cinema-Scope by Budd Boetticher, a group of horsemen ride in mid-shot, the camera tracking back across a desert with a high ridge of sand in the background. Some small objects like dead trees come into view on top of the ridge. The conventional audience waits for a close-up that does not come: those objects are not dead trees, for they begin to move. Horses with Indians riding them. And the chase is on. When did you first see these objects? Before or after you saw the leading cowboy stiffen? Here the director is not leading a passive audience by the hand, showing it only what he wants it to see. Here the audience is on its own.

Again in *Le Amiche* (1955) Michelangelo Antonioni demonstrated the *plan-séquence* and montage. In a series of *plan-séquences* on a beach he manoeuvres his nine or ten characters in the foreground, mid and background with masterly effect. There is an unusually small number of shots in the whole film and some stunning examples of montage between shot and shot, one for instance where a desperate girl, already a failed suicide, runs away from the man who has rebuffed her, down the dark, narrow street in the night into the distance—fade out—fade in on bright morning looking down from a height on to a quayside where a body lies on a stretcher. We never see the face: we never approach. But we know.

The silent film came of age with its subduing of space, the sound film is maturing with the taming of time. Griffith in using the flashback toyed with time but he was unsuccessful in his attempts to tame it in *Intolerance* and had to fall back on the narrative title in his unwieldy efforts to make his way among the four epochs which his four episodes involved. The film, silent or sound, has no past or future tense, only the present. It is the nature of the image which tells you at which period of time you are now present.

This ambiguity of the presentness of past and future is one of the elements, the principal shock effects, of montage towards which Eisenstein had been stretching in *October*, but he had needed the sound track to eliminate the titling, itself too clumsily informative to shock the emotions.

As Phase Three got into its stride, this asset was rediscovered and found valid. The first to react to the possibilities were the young Italians, led by Antonioni, Fellini, and later Rosi. Neo-realism was waning with the circumstances of which it was a true reflection. And now people could be more contemplative. The anecdote was being superseded by a more analytical approach to the post-war problems which had altered the course of all their lives.

As Antonioni has said, reviewing de Sica's masterpiece *The Bicycle Thieves* some years later, it is no longer enough for a film to describe a Sunday's search for a bicycle stolen from an unemployed billposter who needs it for his new job. One wants to know the *man*. Neo-realism meticulously explored surfaces: it never probed beneath the skin.

Hostility from trade and government, which I described earlier, drove Vittorio de Sica into total conformity from the mid-1950s onwards and now his gallant, fighting contribution to the neo-realist movement is largely forgotten by those who live from day to day and to whom an artist is only as good as his most recent film.

It was difficult at first for the audience to adjust to the revolution introduced by Antonioni. His early films had been conventional narratives in substance, but as he assimilated the new flexibilities of cinema which arose naturally with the widening of the image, he found these were a means to explore more deeply into the revelation of character. He began to renounce the incident, to minimize the action which had been the chief asset of cinema and to develop introspection, reflecting the depths of his own character and experience. He is one of those rare film-makers of whom it is true to say that

Louis Malle (1932-    )

Jacques Tati (1908-    )

Claude Chabrol (1930-    )

before studying his films it is rewarding to study his life. It is only then, for example, that one can appreciate his sturdy balance, courage, and sense of humour and look for them in his work.

While during the war Rossellini accommodated himself to Fascism and Fellini lived alongside it, Antonioni came near to starvation rather than support it in his journalism. He lacked the private means and family influence which shielded Visconti, who was equally outspoken in opposition.

Antonioni continued to avoid compromise and in 1960 he presented at the Cannes Festival *L'Avventura*, a film which turned the fashionable audience into a mob of ill-wishers. This is a film of declared introspection in which the movement is slow and the only progress comes with the sharp probing and dissection of character set physically in the insistent presence of place. His intense absorption in architecture and painting shows in every camera set-up, for the environment around his people is chosen as much to illuminate as to frame them.

It was not long before the opinion of that first audience was reversed. Five years later his financial resources were reinforced by a contract with Metro-Goldwyn-Mayer, under which it is hoped he retains creative free-

**Louis Malle**
An acute and sensitive observer who readily tries his hand at many kinds of film

**Claude Chabrol**
*The problem of the cinéaste is twofold: to convey his thoughts to the greatest number, a technical problem; and, secondly, to analyse the structure of truth*

**Jacques Tati**
*The best French comic since Max Linder*
— Georges Sadoul

**Georges Franju**
*Black humour; but . . . what pleases me is anything that is fearful, tender, and poetic*

**Georges Franju (1912-   )**

dom.[1] His intellectual approach is coupled with an austere attitude to acting, of which he has no personal experience, making it harder for him and for his actors to achieve a comfortable performance. In this he differs markedly from his contemporary Federico Fellini, who in the year of *L'Avventura* shocked the social and religious establishments of Italy with his latest and most extrovert film *La Dolce Vita*. Subsequently, while Antonioni continued to cling to chronological reality, Fellini more and more translated his experience of life into dream and fantasy, particularly in his masterpiece *8½* (1963), totally rejecting the neo-realism from which he had sprung. And his experience of acting exuberantly draws out matching performances from professionals and amateurs alike in settings which reflect the Italian tradition of lavish spectacle. There is no physical asset, no trick of cinema that is beyond Fellini's reach.

[1] Antonioni's first film for M-G-M, *Blow Up* (1968), was launched in the art houses and proved to be so successful with the *film* audience that it was released to the *movie* audience in the big, popular cinemas, again with outstanding success. And so his second film, *Zabriskie Point* (1970), was screened first in the *movie* houses, by-passing the discriminating *film* audience whose discernment can build up a more sensitive climate of opinion. As a result, because the film to date has not been a money-spinner in the big cinemas, it has failed to reach the more discerning audience in the art houses.

**Chris Marker**
1921–
For him the age of the image is here. But that doesn't mean that we should sacrifice the word to the image. To him the commentary is almost fundamental

**Jean Rouch**
1917–
Began as an ethnographer and is now the apostle of *cinéma vérité*, the film that doesn't cheat if it can help it

During the 1950s, apart from the austere and sparse works of Robert Bresson—and sparser still, the delicate pantomimes of Jacques Tati—the French cinema had fallen into a rut. But for those who were looking for signs they were to be found among the students of the film school IDHEC,[1] in the cascade of stimulating programmes of silent as well as sound films that was bombarding the screen of Henri Langlois' Cinémathèque française, in the critical columns of film periodicals and the lay press, and above all in the originality of the best French short films, alongside which feature film production, playing for safety against American competition, appeared stagnant.

Thirty years earlier, after the First World War, a similar situation in feature film production had provoked a wave of *avant-garde* cinema backed by private patronage. Now in 1957 the pattern began to repeat itself. Private family wealth made it possible for a few young enthusiasts to make their first feature-length films on a modest scale and these were successful enough for the industry to promote equally competent but less wealthy film-makers from short to feature film production. In the first category were Louis Malle (industrial), François Truffaut (film distribution), Claude Chabrol (pharmaceutical), and Jean-Luc Godard (Swiss banking). In the second group were Alain Resnais, Agnes Varda, Jacques Demy, Georges Franju, Chris Marker, and a host of others. In five years the formula became decadent: a notion on a sheet of paper and no previous experience were the sole qualifications by which some hundreds of worthless projects were judged to deserve financing. Nevertheless the cream of the films of the new wave established their makers in solid and continuing careers, and if twenty-five worthwhile films survived, that is no less than the record of the whole period of Italian neo-realism.

The influences which provoked this movement were healthy. The film-makers had learnt to concentrate on subjects within their own experience, to avoid adaptations from the novel or the play, and in this they far outshone the 'angry young men' of the contemporary British cinema, few of whose sources were original to the screen. These Frenchmen were bourgeois born and bred and refused to adopt the kitchen-sink environment at second-hand, another characteristic of most of their British contemporaries. As liberals they equally rejected the outworn colonialism to which the French conservatives were clinging as evidence of greatness, particularly in Algeria at that time.

But this is all these French film-makers had in common. For the rest they exploited all the less expensive tools of modern cinema, including those which the French ethnographer Dr. Jean Rouch was causing to be evolved for the

[1] Institut d'Hautes Études Cinématographiques.

**Robert Bresson
1907–
Another lone film-maker**

**NEW WAVE—FRANCE**

benefit of his own reportages in Africa and elsewhere.[1] This is the equipment described earlier on page 61: the lightweight hand-held camera, the tiny microphone, the tape recorder slung from the shoulder, all linked by radio; and the ultra-sensitive negative emulsion which can record an exposure in normal room lighting.

The richness of the French new wave lies in its diversity of subject and style. While the films of François Truffaut have become more and more conventional, those of Louis Malle and Alain Resnais retain their constant individuality, Malle content to follow the conservative line while Resnais tests the flexibility of the medium with the sureness of a master, though as his powers grow his methods become simpler. Resnais is probably the most advanced practitioner of film-editing today, and this skill accompanied by his dominant interest in the art of acting finally unites the two streams of influence which derived from the work of D. W. Griffith, the Eisenstein stream, and the Stroheim–Renoir stream. All that Resnais lacks is the fortuitous backing of private means which has helped to stabilize Chabrol, Godard, Malle, and Truffaut. In order to survive in cinema a film-maker must increase in stature, never putting a foot wrong. With private capital to back him he can take risks with less punity, picking and choosing without the anxiety of deadlines, the need of basic pay. Resnais' first four feature films, *Hiroshima mon amour* (1959), *L'Année dernière à Marienbad* (1961), *Muriel* (1963), and *La Guerre est finie* (1966) have won him the reputation of being a leading figure in the progressive manipulation of cinema. He works in collaboration, taking material from established writers; but he influences that material from the start. And he continues to mould it, or distil it, in new ways. We are now too close to the results to judge them dispassionately. We can, though, recommend them as worthy of our time.

From his first feature film *À bout de Souffle* (1959) onwards Godard has accomplished apparent miracles in the capture of improvised action and speech in the busiest, most public surroundings. But for him and his cameraman and his sound recordist it was child's play compared with the ingenuity and pertinacity required to use the cumbersome apparatus of a generation earlier. And Godard would never have tried to do what he has done without the stimulus of the screenings of those earlier films which he had been privileged to study at the Cinémathèque in Paris.

[1] Similar equipment was being perfected in the U.S.A. at the demand of television reporters; the French term for this kind of work is *cinéma-vérité*, the Americans call it direct cinema. It all began with Dziga Vertov and his kino-eye on one side of the world and with Robert Flaherty on the other. But while the Americans, following Vertov, aimed to catch life unawares, the French tended to use it more self-consciously: they pre-arranged the happenings with their strong sense of economy, while the Americans in the effort to be more honest expended miles of material in the hope of catching a moment of golden spontaneity.

Whatever may be said about Godard as an artist, and we are now beginning to deal with events too recent for definitive judgement,[1] his sense of economy has been a beneficial discipline in his work. Godard the non-conformist has had the good sense to reject the offers of the conventional international set and to preserve his early real freedom by choosing subjects within the idiom and the economic bounds of his first efforts. Rarely has he committed more than one hundred thousand dollars into the budget of a film.[2]

Incidentally, there is a genuine problem for the budding film-maker. If he has had some success with his first film he can very easily get enmeshed in a world which can do strange things to him, his career, his future. There is no influence more stiflingly bourgeois than that of the international set in show business whose values too many members of the public aspire to emulate. People who regard brain and imagination as the sole elements requisite to film-making are sadly ignorant of the facts. Character and a goal are equally

[1] Any current estimate of Godard's work is out-of-date as soon as another of his films appears.
[2] *Jean-Luc Godard* par Jean-Luc Godard: Collection des Cahiers du Cinéma, Éditions Pierre Belfond, Paris, 1968. *The Films of Jean-Luc Godard* (ed. Ian Cameron), Movie Paperbacks, Studio Vista, London, 1967. *Godard*, by Richard Roud, Secker and Warburg, London, 1967.

## NEW WAVE—FRANCE

*far left*
**Jean-Luc Godard**
1930–
The quality of a heart in conflict
with a sharp anarchic mind which
sees the world from a pessimistic
viewpoint

*right*
**François Truffaut**
1932–
directing **Jeanne Moreau**
(1928–     ) in *Jules et Jim*:
*I make films to realize my
adolescent dreams, to do a bit of
good for myself and perhaps
other people. For me films are a
form of writing. For me it will
always be an entertainment
where it is forbidden to bore the
audience, or to appeal to only
part of the audience*
*below*
**Alain Resnais**
1922–
*Meticulously selecting and
respecting his writers, he puts
his own seal on his films as the
true author*

necessary. Character, infinite effortless egotism, and a built-in resistance movement against the killing competition, the shallowness, and the pervading cynicism are essential attributes together with the ability to recognize among this welter of self-sufficiency any presence of truth and generosity. That these temptations can even affect production in the nationalized industry of a totalitarian state is demonstrated in the Czech film *The Fifth Horseman is Fear* (1968). In order to gain a wide international market the Czech industry accepted the condition imposed by the Italian impresario Carlo Ponti that the version of this film for export should contain additional sequences set in Czech brothels which were not included in the original script and do not form part of the Czech version of the film. The job is done skilfully enough and it cannot be apparent to the average viewer that the film is more valid without them.[1]

There is a precedent for this distortion, the opposite of mutilation. During the 1930s when censorship was more rigid, French producers found that studios in South America were buying French romantic films for the South American market, cutting out the fade-outs which occurred at censorable situations and continuing the action with doubles replacing the missing players. The practice was only discouraged by more stringent contracts and subsequent vigilance.[2]

There was a period which ended during the First World War, when the successful artist in film could retain his artistic and financial independence. In those days income tax was still low enough for the artist to retain the vast majority of his earnings, sufficient indeed to finance his own films with his own private means. Charles Chaplin is the sole surviving film-maker from those days. He and his colleagues set up the United Artists Corporation to retain control of their own distribution. In an effort to work more freely, the so-called underground film movement aims to distribute their own product co-operatively rather than to allocate it to specialized distributors. But, like antique dealing, film distribution has formed its own establishment with its own code of behaviour, and sooner or later the non-conformists are worn down by the competitive effort to beat their established rivals and tend to join them instead.

The third phase of cinema was bound to develop faster in the capitalist than in the socialist countries. The latter have always been hampered by lack of foreign currency to purchase equipment that is not directly committed to national defence, nor have they been competitively forced to develop their own. They have also been dominated by the wayward dictatorship of the party line, which must be toed or else.

[1] In 1970 the original Czech version was on release in Britain, the Ponti one in the U.S.A.
[2] See note on p. 108.

Nationalization of film industries came to Czechoslovakia, Poland, and Yugoslavia in 1945 and to Bulgaria, Hungary, and Rumania in 1948. It took these nations at least ten further years to adopt a system originally conceived by the Czechs in 1945, competitive enough to stimulate imaginative work about their own problems. Under state censorship it was safer to make boring films about the not-so-recent war in which the villain is always the foreigner. These films, pedestrian in style and content, were rejected even by their conformist populations.

At the time of the unrest in 1956 in Hungary and elsewhere the controllers of the nationalized cinema industries took stock of the situation and instigated production groups around production personalities, in competition, allowing those congenial to each other to gravitate together. There was enough success to dissuade emigration on any marked scale, despite temptations from abroad arising out of increased sales and prestige.

Two institutions spurred on the new movement in socialist as in some capitalist countries: the film school and the film festival. The idea of the film school was invented by totalitarians and therefore was suspect in the free world. The first schools were set up in Moscow (1919), Rome (1935), and Potsdam (1935). Then the idea became associated with maintaining national identity—in occupied Paris (1943), at Lodz in the ruins of Poland (1947), and at Potsdam in East Germany, which inherited the school set up under the Nazis. The movement spread among the satellite states of Eastern Europe, where, however, nationalized industries put a brake on free expression. In Madrid too a new school was hampered by Fascist controls. In western and Asiatic countries the movement began after the Second World War with the advantage of greater freedom of ideas in theoretical study and practical work, once each had found its particular appropriate scope. The socialist schools were hampered by political influences which deliberately separated the function of script-writing from that of direction and editing, discouraging the pursuit of film-making as a single art from the original idea to the first performance. This was considered, and still is by conservative Communists, to be far too individualistic for the common good. It remains the heart and soul of a film education in the rest of the world.

A sufficient film school can in two or three years teach the student the technology which will take him eight years to acquire haphazardly in the narrow confines of the film industry. (And he would need luck as to where his time in industry had been spent.) On completing the course at a school he should be able to embark on film-making at the age of greatest vigour. Graduates in any profession have yet to learn a great deal. But even considered on the practical level a man or woman whose talents and knowledge have had some appraisal is less likely to be the blind gamble for their first commercial employer than they are at the moment. And they can reasonably be expected to inject into their commercial work vitality and fresh ideas thought out in the relative tranquillity of a period of study-training.

A recent extension of this idea is already showing promising results in the U.S.A. Within two years of its foundation in 1967 the American Film Institute set up a centre for advanced film studies to serve as a bridge between film school or university on the one hand and a career in film production, criticism, or study on the other hand, maintaining contact between the beginner and the established professional, and also providing a haven for professionals to refresh themselves with new approaches to unfamiliar branches of their profession. It is hoped that if and when a national film school is founded in Britain its policy will lean more towards advanced studies than towards duplicating efforts already in full exercise elsewhere.

This system of filtering new blood and fresh ideas into the industry is balanced at the other end of the process by the film festival, where the finished product is seen, weighed up, and publicized by international experts. The competitive element generates excitement and suspense, adding some gaiety to a basically hard-headed commercial enterprise. If favourable publicity is given to a film and particularly if it wins a prize, it acquires a valuable asset in the market bargaining. The international juries of about a dozen people from the many branches of the industry are invited by a committee, some of whom probably function as organizers over a number of years. Not all the film festivals are competitive and commercial and they can develop endearing local flavours and idiosyncrasies.

To launch a film through an established system of distribution, the American for instance, entails at the very least, expenditure half as much again as the cost of production. Without the help of such a system the cost of distribution can expand as much as ten times the cost of production when the distribution is not being shared among a group of films. It is here that the film festival comes into its own. In the two weeks' span of the normal festival a buyer, usually a film distributor, can evaluate more films than would be possible in three months' travel. And he can check his views against those of dozens of critics, members of the industry, journalists, professionals and amateurs, people with a good nose for a film. Most important, while propaganda issued by the producers continually makes assumptions which vary considerably from any absolute assessment, in private conversations there can be a rationale, shades of objectivity. For the artist the variety of nationalities provides exotic reaction to his work which is not to be found in the field of domestic film criticism.

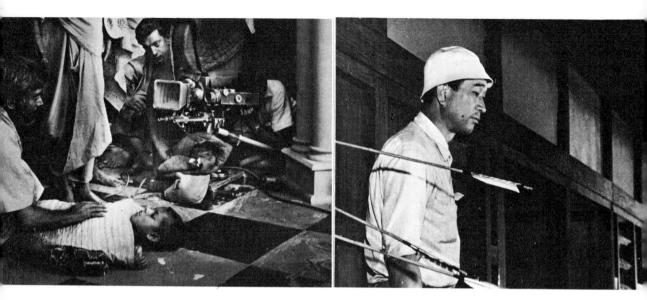

## COMPLETE FILM-MAKERS

The major international festivals are those of Venice, set up in 1932 to glorify Fascism, Cannes (1946) which quickly developed into a frank trade fair, Berlin (1950) as part of the campaign to re-establish the German identity of West Berlin and which therefore has political connotations such as Venice lost after the war, and Moscow (1959) which alternates with that of Karlovy Vary in Czechoslovakia: these last two are the main festivals of the Communist bloc.

Important festivals of shorter films are held at Venice, at Oberhausen and Mannheim in West Germany, and at Tours in France. All over the world minor festivals proliferate, at present amounting to some hundred and twenty, some competitive, some not (as in London), some specializing in a particular category of film. Inevitably, in every sense of the word, there has arisen a group of persons whose only claim to notoriety is their habitual attendance at these functions and their skill at ignoring every point other than those of the smallest interest. But there is no doubt that in a world without festivals the development of cinema would be as chaotic as in a world without film schools.

To take an example, the Asian cinema was ignored in the western world until the Japanese, freed from American military occupation, began looking for wider markets and submitted Kurosawa's film *Rashomon* to the Venice festival of 1951 where it won the first prize, the golden lion. Japanese films won six more prizes at European festivals during the next years and Japanese films of appropriate quality began to compete successfully in the American and European markets.

In 1956 Satyajit Ray, a Bengali (a student of Jean Renoir) showed his film *Pather Panchali* at Cannes, and its sequel *Aparajito* at Venice in 1957 (another golden lion). At these festivals his work, a break-through, swept aside the western assumption that all Indian film-making was parochial and displayed accomplishment of international stature.

We are approaching the point where the reader takes over. During the 1960s the situation of cinema sharply divided the mean-minded from the generous. For the mean, it was a time when attendance at circuit cinemas and consequently the number of these cinemas continued to decline. For the generous, it was the time when the art house and the ciné-club movements spread all over the world and when the numbers of non-conformist film-makers proliferated to a degree unforeseen before the technical innovations of Phase Three began to become available. For the mean, Hollywood, and therefore the film in general, declined with the closing of studios and the brash intrusion of television, while for the generous the film was developing beyond the need for the artifice of studios and into the possibility of working in surroundings formerly inaccessible. For the mean, the commerce of cinema was becoming more exacting, demanding higher standards of intelligence and education than the old brigade possess. For the generous, the cinema was coming of age, a challenge no longer beneath the dignity of the fine and performing arts which are older by so many thousands of years.

Ironically, television, now intruding on cinema as cinema had intruded on the living theatre seventy years earlier, lacks the great advantage that tested cinema in its early days, that of starting life as a silent medium. Television never had to fight its way through cinema's Phase One to win its spurs, the gift of sound. Television, born with its spurs on, after an uncomfortable birth is developing through a comparatively simple childhood, with short term needs more dominant than long term potentials.

By the beginning of the 1970s, to revert to Professor Huaco's theory of the four factors, there is less to worry about in the first three factors than ever before. It is the fourth factor that needs attention. Here commerce is correct in its diagnosis, but the remedies proposed may kill more than they cure.

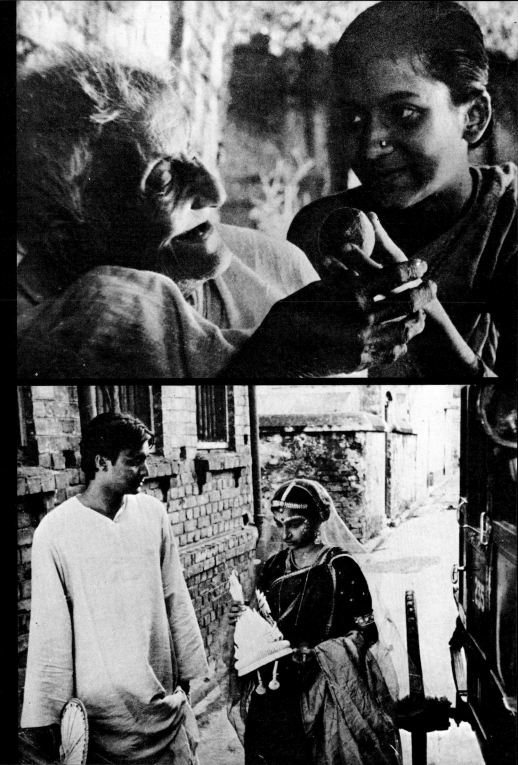

Satyajit Ray
**PATHER PANCHALI**
1955

**Influenced by Jean Renoir, a book illustrator films a book and the word takes second place**

Satyajit Ray
**THE WORLD OF APU**
1959

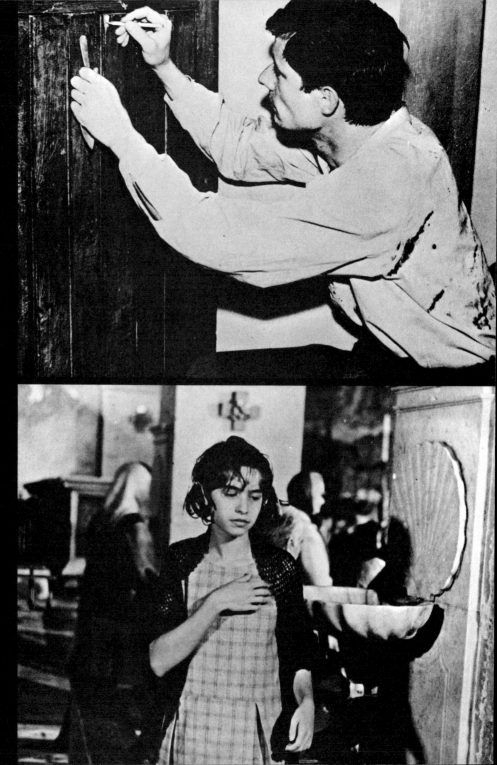

**Robert Bresson
UN CONDAMNÉ À
MORT S'EST ÉCHAPPÉ**
1956

**Bresson the austere:
his tools, the non-
actor and the
significant detail**

**Robert Bresson
MOUCHETTE**
1967

Alain Resnais
**L'ANNÉE DERNIÈRE
À MARIENBAD**
1961
with Delphine Seyrig

**Time manipulated by
control over thesis,
acting, composition,
and editing**

Alain Resnais
**MURIEL**
1963
with Delphine Seyrig

Jean Rouch
Edgar Morin
**CHRONIQUE D'UN
ÉTÉ**
1961
**Cinéma Vérité**

**Realism in the new
wave in France**

Louis Malle
**LE FEU FOLLET**
1963

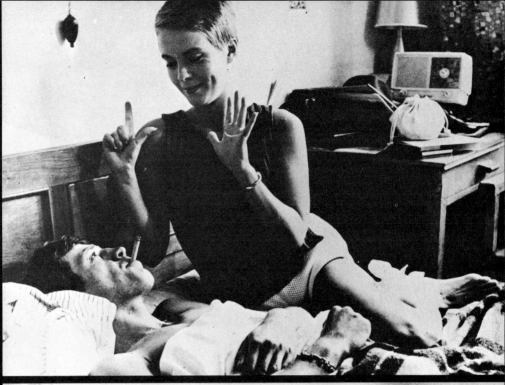

Jean-Luc Godard
**À BOUT DE SOUFFLE**
1959
with Jean Seberg and
Jean-Paul Belmondo

**How long is a comet's tale?**

Jean-Luc Godard
**WEEKEND**
1968

Ingmar Bergman
**WILD STRAWBERRIES**
1958
with Victor Sjöstrom
and Ingrid Thulin

The modern
'chamber film'

Ingmar Bergman
**THROUGH A GLASS
DARKLY**
1961
with Harriet Andersson

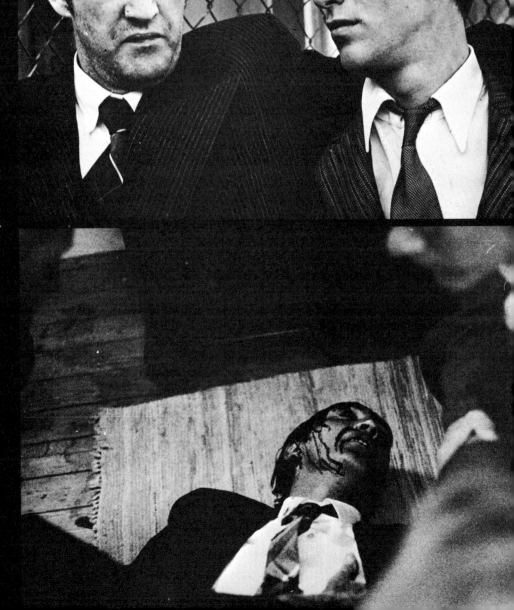

**Bo Wideberg
RAVEN'S END**
1964

**The new deal in
Sweden encourages a
new generation**

**Bo Wideberg
ADALEN 31**
1968

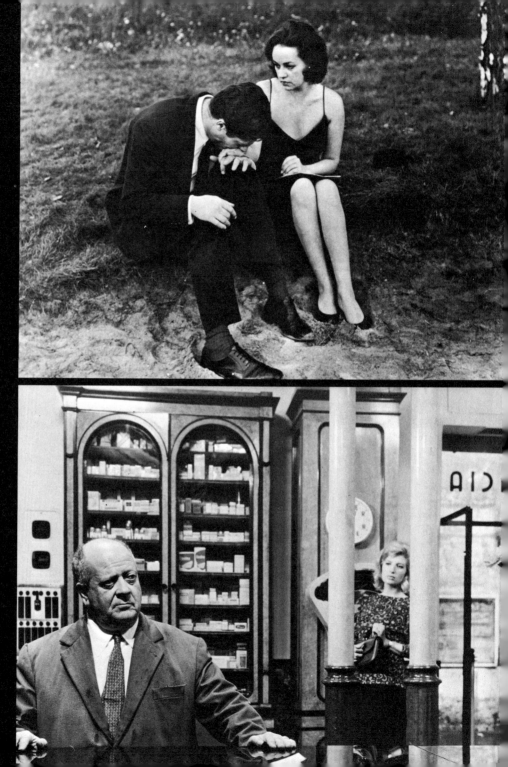

Michelangelo Antonioni
**LA NOTTE**
1961
with Jeanne Moreau and
Marcello Mastrianni

**After Neo-Realism
the counterpoint of
personalities in their
world of custom and
artefacts**

Michelangelo Antonioni
**L'ECLISSE**
1962
with Monica Vitti

Federico Fellini
**I VITELLONI**
1953

**Exuberant,
autobiographical
cinema**

Federico Fellini
**OTTO E MEZZO**
1963
**English title '8½'**

Luis Buñuel
**VIRIDIANA**
1961

**Surrealism in fiction
and surrealism in fact**

Andrzej Munk
**PASSENGER**
1963

Jean Vigo
**ZÉRO DE CONDUITE**
1932

**The collapse of
Authority**

Lindsay Anderson
**IF.**
1968

John Schlesinger
**MIDNIGHT COWBOY**
1969
with Jon Voight and
Dustin Hoffman

**Films that shook the
Hollywood
establishment**

Dennis Hopper
**EASY RIDER**
1969
with Peter Fonda and
Dennis Hopper

**Phase Three is still** evolving around us and an assessment of the confluences on the four factors of cinema can only be ephemeral.

The changes wrought by war and politics on the peoples of the world altering the geographical boundaries of nations, the leaven of a growing concern for the quality of all our lives, the explosions in scientific knowledge and in the arts constitute the components of revolution. The eruptions of physical violence, much featured in the indignations of some of the elderly, are a dangerous symptom of frustration at the slow pace of inevitable change. As Joyce Cary, the author, used to say, 'There is always chaos and a lot of dust when you have a big construction job on your hands.' The phenomenon which particularly distinguishes this era from the periods of Phase One and Phase Two is confident youth, increasingly classless and politically-conscious, who ask the questions *how* and *why* to which they reject mass-produced answers.

Against this background there is exploration and discussion of the nature of creative talent, and from this climate we have in fifteen years sporadically seen fine freer films made by artists using the modern versatile tools, films in which expanding techniques have been used to transmute more of the intricacies of day-to-day life on to the cinema screens than have been achieved before.

The audience, who nowadays are those who go to the cinema because they are interested and knowledgeable, offer some hope that vigilantes will group to keep the four factors in balance and to fight the very real threat of a retrograde cinema dominated by television. Because commerce has no interest in the art of film for the most part, apart from money-making on the jack-pot scale, it is quite possible that cinema could become merely a tool of television unless new thinking and caring is applied to the making and showing of films. And this would be an incalculable loss. A film (which can be run over and over again) aimed to enthral millions, can be a force for good and ill, but in either case it is extra-ordinary. Against this huge scale of opportunity a block, small in scale but deadly in potency, threatens a balanced growth of cinema. Under capitalism all ideas on film (talking commercially) are filtered through a minuscule caucus of business men, the establishment which controls distribution and in countries like Britain exhibition as well, and whose aim is to make money. Under Communism and Maoism a caucus also functions with the additional filter of a political censorship.

In the nature of the vagaries of life occasionally a film turned down by commerce surfaces and is received rapturously by a modern audience to the amazement of the caucus to whom it is incomprehensible. And it is the incomprehension of these men, who hold us all enmeshed in their bank balances, which inhibits and imprisons the artists and strangles ideas at birth. Discussion has to be carried on from some mutually understood basis of knowledge and imagination. Opinions can differ but there is the possibility of connecting if people's references have something in common. Attempts at money-making with moronic old formulae as a sole reference can only effect certain death for cinema, because as these ideas do not now make money, commerce will withdraw from film-making on any scale. And though they would no doubt like to make money from new ideas, at this period of time they do not appear to understand what the artists are communicating to the audience. As I said earlier, the abiding problem is to reconcile the conformist needs of commerce with the assets which only the non-conformists can provide.

If the compound that is not something photographed but something on its own, is to live, there will have to be a major transfusion of really imaginative thinking into the organization of the film trade and industry during this Phase Three.

# The Fourth Factor

The first factor is the political and social climate; the second the creative capacity of the artist, and the number of these artists; third, the flexibility of film equipment; and fourth the audience.

The audience is the key to the possibility of the expansion of range open to the artist. Imaginative comprehension of what is on the screen gives continuing life to a creative work. A completed film can be said to exist only when it is on the screen, and non-comprehension of its ideas is as deadly to those ideas as a bullet is to a body.

Artists can transmute the world for us, but the audience is the catalyst with the power to recognize their worth, and only if there is recognition of good work in this young medium will there be continuing employment of those whose work is shown. Where talent is not used and appreciated, it withers away. The catalyst receives in its collective mind provocative additions to the understanding of something new or of new thoughts on old problems, a myriad repercussions. And if this adds up to exploratory thinking, it must, to have any results, be followed by action.

But film criticism is rarely achieved. Just as knowledge and understanding of the long established arts is an element in education (an enrichment of our lives), so should the advantage of knowing something about and understanding cinema (and television) be included in our upbringing. These potent media deserve trained critics. When we do not keep pace with our artists, the best in cinema goes into cold storage, waiting (if the producer has not already had the negative destroyed) as *La Règle du jeu* was shelved from 1939 till 1960. Multiply this situation and a tongue-in-cheek decadence will spread like a cancer and could strangle the medium.

The age group most easily attracted to the many forms of entertainment is that from seventeen to the mid-twenties, between leaving school and the arrival of the first child. A lesser but important number of adults, whose growing children have their own distractions, come under consideration. This older public has transferred its regular attendance at the cinema to watching television; they choose their films from reviews or by word of mouth, they are no longer a passive audience. This increases the cost of exploiting and showing films about which the film trade makes bitter complaint. The task ahead in any nation aiming at a high standard of living requires that a subjective landscape of ideas will be available through all the media of communication, including films; ideas inviting discussion and discrimination, about which people can agree or disagree, but with reasoned thought. This is in the essential long term interest of all. Passiveness signals decay.

There is a growing body of opinion which is now concentrating on the establishment of a good standard of education in primary schools, and certainly this should be the latest age at which to begin guiding children towards a sharpened appreciation of sight and sound. In an ideal world this would already have begun at home. Happenings around them add up to formative discoveries they have not experienced before. Study of the range of cinema on the level of higher education has scarcely begun which means that it has been left far too late; there are exceptions and where there is tuition and practice results have been notable.

The cinema in its seventy-five years seems to have taken a step forward about once in every five years and now reflects adolescent confusions. It is therefore levelling up with its largest audience. This age group, experiencing for the first time the distractions of the permissive society—the overworked phrase which has become a swingdoor between heaven and hell—is confronted with a flood of films made with little technical skill and which stifle with boredom, induced as much by over-exposure and over-indulgence as from the poverty of thought. A bored audience soon becomes a lost audience. The cinema has to grow up, which of course it can, but this is a human state of affairs and only we can alter it.

There is a precedent for a spearhead audience to take matters into its own hands, to become the collective patron of their own twentieth-century art form. A million subscribers—Medici like—can commission a work from an artist and having paid for it at one viewing can place it in distribution and commission another work from the proceeds, if their judgement has been sound enough to justify this course. Two such projects have been achieved in France: Jean Renoir's film mentioned earlier,which was backed by the trade union movement, *La Marseillaise* (1938), and Maurice Cloche's film for Roman Catholic social clubs, *Monsieur Vincent* (1947). Both had a propagandist motive, but there is nothing to prevent the similar promotion of work by, for instance, federations of film societies. There is no difference between a Medici commissioning a statue from Michelangelo and a million members of film societies buying their seats two years in advance to see a film they have commissioned from Antonioni.

An epitome of this situation in cinema in 1969 is the case of the film *If*. Spurned as a project by British financiers, the production was eventually backed by American capital which gave total freedom within its budget to its maker, that uncompromising individualist Lindsay Anderson. Because it had an original script and was played by a cast without a star among them, it had to be publicized on Anderson's name alone, a director with a following but no widely popular record. Its backers presented it in the theatre in London which they fortunately owned, since neither of the two major circuits showed interest. The response of viewers and critics alike was so enthusiastic that a circuit release was hastily arranged with equally successful results, and these were subsequently repeated in other countries in spite of the peculiarly local nature of the British public school system which the film satirizes.

Here we have a case of hopeless conservatism on the part of the national film trade with a hopeful result when the conservatives were proved wrong. And the pay-off is equally ironical: because of the British lack of judgement all the net profits of this American film will be channelled to Wall Street (together with ninety per cent of the rest of the products of British cinema so long as the recent situation prevails).

The reader may claim that here the audience behaved actively and imaginatively and that it is the film trade which was at fault. Certainly, however small has been the British contribution to the developing art of film, our nation was among the first to cultivate the audience.

Back in 1933 the British Film Institute was set up nationally with this exact aim. Within two years the B.F.I. had founded the National Film Archive under its current curator Ernest Lindgren to preserve as much film of value as lay in its power, film to which the active international audience cultivated by the Institute could refer. In 1951 the B.F.I. inaugurated the first National Film Theatre in the world, located in London. During its first thirty years of operation the B.F.I. had to struggle forward with inadequate funds and only recently under its present management has it been able to extend its activities to the provinces with already forty film theatres in operation.

Films like *If* benefit in Britain from the solid, permanent influence of the environment created by the educational services, publications, lectures, screenings, and information services of such an Institute. The British Film Institute Production Fund provided the backing with which Lindsay Anderson and his contemporaries, Karel Reisz, Tony Richardson, and others could make the start in the mid-1950s which they named Free Cinema, a group of films relatively mild as seen from the climate of 1970. But while they have since gained a vital and articulate audience they cannot yet be said to have done more than mildly dent that conservative edifice, commercial cinema monopoly. Films like Dennis Hopper's *Easy Rider* (1969) (disillusioned youth's lament for America's lost freedoms, a film made outside all the existing commercial conventions), and John Schlesinger's *Midnight Cowboy* (1969) (an up-to-the-minute open discussion on age-old subjects which even five years back would have been taboo in the cinema), are dealing hammer blows on a bewildered commercial establishment failing to comprehend why this new freer cinema is sweeping all before it.

We can learn much from one country whose films have scarcely been mentioned here. Sweden, a nation with a population less than that of any one

## THIRD-PHASE BRITISH FILM-MAKERS

*above*
**John Schlesinger**
1925–
Directing **Julie Christie**
(1941–    ) in *Far From the Madding Crowd*

*right*
**Lindsay Anderson**
1923–

*far right*
**Karel Reisz** (in foreground)
1926–

of the world's three largest cities, has a record of creative achievement in cinema which comes close to that of nations five times its size. While larger nations like Holland and Belgium can rarely afford to make more than half a dozen feature films a year, Sweden has consistently clung to an average schedule of some twenty-five a year for most of fifty years. Recently when television and foreign competition threatened this schedule a way was found to sustain the industrial effort and on a high creative level with no lowering of standards of quality.

The physical and economic scale of Swedish productions has always been kept low. Production crews are kept to a minimum, around a dozen craftsmen per feature film. Swedish films can only pay their way with their foreign sales and by avoiding competition with the lavish popular product of larger nations. The Swedes are the most literate nation on earth and Swedish films so far as possible are aimed at a more intelligent audience than those of, say, America or Britain and are made on a far more modest scale. By aiming at a smaller audience they have not incurred the opposition of foreign traders, though the German and American industries have lured many a Swedish artist to emigrate.

A career in Swedish cinema is a choice for the dedicated, not for the money-grabber. There can be no artificial forcing up of salaries as a measure of

competence, as happens in the rat race of commercial cinema elsewhere. At the same time there is probably more steady employment for the devotees and the competent than elsewhere.

Neutrality in two world wars certainly helped to maintain a steady flow of product. But more than once the effort has been slowed down by outside interference. During the 1920s when Hollywood was importing foreign artists to enrich its waning silent film, Sweden was impoverished by the emigration of its two leading directors, Victor Sjöstrom and Mauritz Stiller, and of two rising players, Greta Garbo and Lars Hansen. And before it had time to recover, Hollywood introduced the talking picture. The Swedish language market was too small to amortize even a modest Swedish sound film of any quality. Indeed for this reason a Swedish process for recording sound on film had been suppressed in 1921. By 1929 the Swedish industry had to import the German Tobis system to survive and the only solution was to make 'quickies', shallow, utility films of the cheapest possible kind whose only asset was their Swedish dialogue. For in those early days of sound film sub-titles translating foreign languages were kept to a minimum, merely synopsising the story line. It was a vicious circle from which finally the Second World War tugged them free.

Export offers came again from belligerent countries and after the war specialized cinemas began to be established in developed countries to cope with the demand of a small, more intelligent audience for alien, less predictable films which were entirely in the best tradition of the Swedish cinema. Now for the past twenty-five years the growing art house market has been receptive of the best films the Swedes have to offer. It was only after the impact of television on the home market (a reduction from 70,000,000 attendances in 1956 to 50,000,000 in 1960, for example) that production had to begin again to watch its step.

Working in the theatre during the winter and on a film in the summer, Ingmar Bergman and his players could scarcely put a foot wrong. But the older generation, Gustaf Molander and Alf Sjoberg for instance, ceased to find backing and newcomers like Bo Wideberg, Vilgot Sjöman, and Jorn Donner had to tread warily.

It was then that an immigrant journalist from Vienna, Harry Schein, a member of the audience indeed, took a hand. In brief, he talked the Swedish Government and film industry into a new frame of mind: to grasp the nettle of the art of the film instead of brushing it aside to avoid being stung, as the rest of the world persisted in doing. By curbing the physical ambitions of cinema, restricting production budgets to an average equivalent of £50,000 or $150,000, Swedish cinema had managed to survive with a modicum of

## COMPLETE FILM-MAKERS—
SWEDEN

*above*
**Ingmar Bergman**
1918–

*right*
**Bo Wideberg**
1930–

*far right*
**Alf Sjoberg**
1930–

international sales because within this modest range the creative effort had been encouraged to produce works of high quality.

Mr. Schein asked two questions: why not encourage this art with the same kind of subsidies as support opera, ballet, and drama? Why not consider film to be a cultural activity as much as an industrial product?

The response came quickly. In 1963 the Swedish Film Institute was founded to administer funds derived not from the state but from a tax of 10% on tickets sold in all cinemas giving six or more performances a week. The annual sum amounts to some £900,000 or a little over $2,000,000. The money is divided in the following ratios: 30% (like the Eady[1] fund in Britain) is divided among Swedish films in proportion to their income in Sweden. 18% is paid out as prizes for quality in Swedish long films and 2% for quality in Swedish short films.

Then comes the recognition of the art of the film. 15% is shared among films whose high standards of quality deny them adequate returns at the box-

[1] The British Film Fund, brain-child of the late Sir Wilfred Eady, is a levy on the sale of all tickets in British cinemas and amounts to an annual sum of between four and five million pounds. The fund is paid to the producers of legally British films shown in those cinemas during the year in proportion to the gross amount that each film has earned once the cinemas have taken their share. The fund has encouraged a high proportion of American finance (as much as 90%) into British production. In Hollywood and New York such films are counted, as American films made wholly on foreign locations.

office in Sweden, acting as a subsidy on the lines accorded to opera and ballet. But the profits they earn abroad are their own affair.

Next comes the encouragement of development in the medium: 30% is devoted to the national film school and the national film audience, film societies, archive, research, and educational study. And 5% is for promotion of the Swedish film abroad, in publications, at film festivals, Swedish film weeks, lecture tours, and the like.

Judgement of quality is in the hands of a jury of seven, with two members changing every year. The scheme was so successful that within two years the Danes followed suit.

Today business-men will tell you that in spite of the Swedish Film Institute plan the Swedish industry is largely kept alive by making pornographic films, to which one may reply that were it not for the existence of the plan there would probably be no Swedish film industry in existence at all. When one contemplates the films which the plan has made possible, films like *Elvira Madigan* (1967), *Adalen 31* (1968) (both by Bo Wideberg), and *Hugo and Josefin* (1967), by Kjell Grede on the one hand, and *I am Curious Yellow* (1967) on the other, one can only salute the freedom accorded to the Swedish film-maker.

The business-men will also tell you that such a system, dependent on the opinions of a jury whose judgement of quality is accepted by the rest of the nation, is unthinkable in Britain or in America. Times change. A generation ago Covent Garden Opera House was a dance hall reluctantly handed over to opera for only six weeks in each summer. Since the war, with a subsidy from the State which now amounts to one and a quarter million pounds sterling a year, the theatre has become a full-time opera house with its own ballet company. It is all a matter of personalities. The changing of the climate of opinion creates the opportunity, which in turn finds the people to carry out the pioneering.

We have begun to breed an active, discriminating audience, the fourth factor. It is for them to study the first factor, the times we live in, and with their own support to encourage the other two factors, the artists and the means the artists need to employ. Who can deny that by the turn of the next century the moving image may not be recognized in America and Britain as a cultural activity worthy of subsidy like the other performing arts? What began as an entertainment industry will have developed an art within itself, a pearl in an oyster, and only the oyster can know the pain induced by the growing pearl.

**Envoi**

In the space available in a short summary (before the origins and early struggles of cinema become too befogged by distance) one can only outline a few facts as an index to further research and particularly conservation. I have deliberately kept my outline at ground level. All of us will follow the makers of films, the variations of technical possibilities, and will respond to the impact of ideas which are magnetic to our personal sensibilities.

By this approach I have underlined a fact of immediate pertinence at this juncture in time. Whether one appreciates the irony that so much of the 'development' of cinema has been tied to the necessity that it should make millions for some is irrelevant. It is a basic fact against which the future of that pearl in the oyster, the art of the film, has to be viewed. Before too much philistinism drags cinema in the wrong direction, how can this fund of know-how be best used and diffused? In what new ways could work be organized? Could co-operative finance allow greater freedom? These are the directions in which sight lines to be explored and acted on in these immediate years need to be established.

Twenty years ago it was essential to visit a concert hall to hear a long musical work complete and uninterrupted. Nowadays we can buy our concerts on long-playing records and listen to them in our own time. The film cassette or cartridge on a video-player plugged into a television set, is already a fact. More ambitious machines are becoming available which record films and television programmes and play them back. As in the early days of colour photography, of sound film, and of television, there are rival systems which will have to become compatible so that they play back all video-recordings, just as record-players must take any make of gramophone record if machine or disc is to have a wide sale. And, as has been the case with colour film and sound film, the system that will prevail must accommodate every surviving variety of video-recording with the least effort and the least deterioration of the cartridge. This is the physical problem.

The solution of the mental problem may usher in the Fourth Phase of cinema for it will mark the acceptance of the notion, anathema to the antiquated film trade, that the work must be imaginative enough to justify more than one viewing, to inspire many of us to hire it for further viewing or to purchase it outright.

The conundrum posed by the existence of machines that record as well as being able to play back is in the fact of universal piracy. The bootlegging of films and recordings has always been a headache. What is the legal position when millions of machines are bought for the purpose of making electronic recordings of programmes transmitted for performance under copyright?

In the early days of cassettes we will view these on our television sets. But just as Hi-Fi sound is the goal of the fanatic for reproducing sound with fidelity, we must eventually project cassette films on to our own screen areas, which will have adjustable borders so that we receive the picture in the aspect ratio in which it was shot. The problem of scale and size will, for some time, only be solved by attending our communal cinemas with their large screens.

The sooner we can possess our films and regard them in the same category as paintings, books, records, the better. The level of educated intelligence is rising rapidly. Those who make films must keep up with populations numbered in millions who will buy film cassettes: films to be seen over and over again, treasured as, say, a collection of paintings. By the experience of the course of the older arts, among the lollipops there will be good meat. Advertising will move into a different groove. The present narrow field of distribution will be radically widened, and film exhibition in draughty, out-of-date buildings will vanish. The prospect almost dazzles. Quality films needing to be seen on a big screen, and gaining something from community pleasure, will continue to be made. And these films could be shown in modest buildings constructed for human comfort, that are more an attractive combination of meeting place, restaurant-bar, and space for a leisurely talking shop than anything which is usual now.

The whole world stands poised on the opening up of communication. Cinema and television are key media. As each new medium arrives the older forms grow in importance to greater numbers of people. Old and new dovetail to provide a stimulating background to the multiple modes of life. With the increasing automating and computerizing of the dreary chores of modern living there cannot be too many channels for the dissemination of ideas, the life enhancers, which are going to be needed by us all.

# Appendix I

## The Delineation of the Moving Image: Comment and Criticism

There are some points concerning film study that I find important and would like to clarify.

The eye should be trained to as great a degree as our education now trains the ear.

Only since the Second World War has the training of the eye for other than utilitarian purposes begun to be considered in our system of education. In the period of the First World War when I was at school, eyes were apparently only for finding one's way, reading, and writing. The discovery of the magic of colour and line, composition, visual rhythm was an accidental event, something individual.

If the situation is improving, certain credit must be given to the power of the cinema, the one-eyed medium which when it is forced into reliance on the components of literature and the theatre to hold one's fullest interest is the more liable to fail. It discloses a new province of expression for which our eyes and ears have to be trained. A person unused to viewing film on a screen is physically unable to follow the visual continuity and so of course much less the content. The remarkable work in training vision which has begun in our primary schools is good; and here and there in schools for later age groups some study of cinema and television has been introduced. But, at the moment, students arrive at the university with only an inkling of the subject and are obliged to undertake intensive discipline to benefit from the increasing prospect before them, a continent where there are as yet too few teachers to guide them. There is therefore an urgent future for combining teaching or tutoring with making films, an invaluable counter-balance between taking-in and giving-out.

The convention of attaching the language of other media to the study of the moving image should be rejected. If you dip into a shelf of books on cinema and television, shots are referred to as the equivalent of words, scenes as sentences, sequences as chapters; the authors write about the grammar and syntax of the film, a new medium of story telling, of narrative. The whole subject is hooked on to literature as a junior appendage. There is a university drama department here, an English department there, a communications department in an American university, each housing a tentative exploration of cinema and/or television. It is all an attempt to justify a resemblance to other media which is in fact casual.

Moving image is an unattractive phrase but it does embrace both cinema and television. For reasons of commerce the two inventions have been separated and promoted in an atmosphere of rivalry, even of bitterness. Television is an extension of an existing field, a different method of projecting the picture and an additional one of receiving the image. Those who practise and understand the one can practise and understand the other with variations in emphasis of function, not an absolute difference, creatively speaking. Increasingly television programmes are being pre-recorded on film or magnetic tape and edited before transmission, which is a basic technique of film-making. The possibilities in further television skills, hardly tapped as yet, do not invalidate this position.

The principal difference at this date between television and cinema is in reception. The one is normally seen by a small group in a room, each person liable to be conscious of his neighbour and therefore self-conscious. In a cinema the individual is relatively anonymous in the darkness.

A reading knowledge of English and French and if possible a third language should be compulsory in the serious study of film. The international literature on our subject is already vast, and there is enough of good quality to make study rewarding. But the rapid changes in the medium push many of the books back from immediate validity to historical interest, vital for research but not necessarily helpful when applied to immediate work. Periodicals should be an important part of the answer, but there is scarcely one with the detachment towards trends in production and in public response; for the most part they explore personalities and review films singly. For them a particular tree is more important than anything that is happening to the forest.

The literature in English is still surpassed in quality by writings in other languages: French, Italian, Russian, and German works cry out for a translation service such as the Hungarian Film Institute provides with its monthly digest of translations from foreign periodicals. Meanwhile we have to read them in the original languages, if we can.

Support for the system of National Film Archives and their international association should be a priority concern for everyone. The twentieth is the first century in which there is the equipment to preserve its image for reference by future centuries. The layman may regard films as a distraction to be seen sporadically at leisure in a cinema. But the majority are produced for information and persuasion, for record and demonstration, as a more vivid method than the written word or the still photograph.

If you imagine space and time as a moving band, infinite into the past and into the future, how much of the past seventy-five years has been reported directly or recreated imaginatively as a distillation of events? An enormous amount of footage; and too much has been allowed to disintegrate, or has been destroyed, thought to be worthless or to be infringing someone's copyright. Anyone who studies cinema positively will have suffered the despair of watching the rights of acknowledged works of value lapse after one or more periods of seven years, the customary time during which a distributor contracts to circulate a foreign film in his business territory. He cannot afford to keep it longer in circulation. Statutory deposit of copies of films in a national archive is too expensive under a system of private enterprise, and at this moment it is only possible in a totalitarian state. Voluntary deposit is haphazard and too often confined to prints scratched and broken by over-use. The solution lies in giving the State archives the right to purchase new prints at choice and the funds to pay for them.

It is a glaring possibility that in a hundred years' time historians will conjecture that the cinema of private enterprise was minuscule compared with the totalitarian output, a myth that can only be destroyed by a collective effort now, before it is too late. No student can afford to ignore this problem of film preservation. It is particularly important to work for the provision of copies to be available for studious analysis, not as heretofore at single screenings but for private scrutiny for weeks on end. They ought to be as accessible as books in a library; and, of course, when we have the equivalent of the literary Penguins in film cassettes, all such organizations will be that much more civilized. And the choice of films should be governed as much by their intrinsic contribution to potentialities as for their merit as successful works in themselves.

Living memory scarcely covers these seventy-five years from the beginning. There is much to do to establish the truth of these times. Cinema is a synthetic medium. The camera does not lie, but it can easily be made to cheat. The sound-track with its synchronous and non-synchronous noises, its choice of music and spoken word, can falsify up to the hilt. There is nothing constant except the sharp memory of accurate observation and integrity in the attempt to pin down the truth.

In this quest fiction illuminates the factual. Though there is a greater quantity of the latter, it could not have afforded to develop without the fiction film's competitive need for change and its greater potential for profit. With the growth of television the factual film is more competitive and profitable, and now in its turn is experimenting with techniques which fiction film is appropriating, including in these the use of improvisation.

As a reflection of contemporary fact, you cannot take the fiction film at its face value.[1] The capacity of those making the film, the adequacy of the

[1] For example, in *Lawrence of Arabia* (1962) the hero rides imposingly with General Allenby into Damascus but in the newsreel he is caught unimportantly in the background.

equipment used, the historical moment of its making, for which audience it was intended, all have to be checked. But often fiction, less accurate in detail, can reveal as vividly as contemporary factual images.

When you have reached this state of appreciation, you will find you have passed from the state of rejecting almost all cinema to that of giving the benefit of the doubt to every scrap of exposed film: to you all film will be innocent until you have proved it guilty.

# Appendix 2

## Objective Narrative, Subjective Personal Statement, and Factual Film

a programme

The following schedules of films used by the Slade Film Department during one year demonstrate the development of two streams of cinema deriving from D. W. Griffith: (1) objective narrative; (2) the subjective personal statement. A third line of film development, the factual film, which stemmed from Eisenstein—who had been influenced by Griffith—was also shown. During one university term a supplement of ten programmes of long and short factual and fictional films was shown in conjunction with five lectures by Mr. A. J. P. Taylor on the subject of the First World War.

### Narrative film

EARLY SHORT FILMS

| | | | |
|---|---|---|---|
| *The Great Train Robbery* | Edwin Porter | U.S.A. | 1903 |
| *The Fall of Troy* | Giovanni Pastrone | Italy | 1910 |
| *A la Conquête du Pôle* | Georges Méliès | France | 1912 |
| *The Exploits of Elaine* | Louis Gasnier | U.S.A. | 1915 |
| *A Night at the Show* | Charles Chaplin | U.S.A. | 1915 |
| *The Massacre* | D. W. Griffith | U.S.A. | 1912 |

*Silent Films*

| | | | |
|---|---|---|---|
| *The Birth of a Nation* | D. W. Griffith | U.S.A. | 1915 |
| *Foolish Wives* | Erich von Stroheim | U.S.A. | 1921 |
| *Greed* | Erich von Stroheim | U.S.A. | 1924 |
| *Le Tournoi* | Jean Renoir | France | 1929 |

150

*Sound Films*

| | | | |
|---|---|---|---|
| *Boudu sauvé des eaux* | Jean Renoir | France | 1932 |
| *Le Crime de Monsieur Lange* | Jean Renoir | France | 1935 |
| *Une partie de campagne* | Jean Renoir | France | 1936 |
| *La Grande Illusion* | Jean Renoir | France | 1937 |
| *La Marseillaise* | Jean Renoir | France | 1938 |
| *La Règle du jeu* | Jean Renoir | France | 1939 |
| *Ossessione* | Luchino Visconti | Italy | 1942 |
| *La Terra trema* | Luchino Visconti | Italy | 1948 |
| *Rome Open City* | Roberto Rossellini | Italy | 1946 |
| *The Bicycle Thieves* | Vittorio de Sica | Italy | 1948 |
| *Umberto D* | Vittorio de Sica | Italy | 1952 |
| *La Signora senza camilie* | Michelangelo Antonioni | Italy | 1953 |
| *Le Amiche* | Michelangelo Antonioni | Italy | 1955 |
| *L'Avventura* | Michelangelo Antonioni | Italy | 1960 |
| *La Notte* | Michelangelo Antonioni | Italy | 1961 |
| *I Vitelloni* | Federico Fellini | Italy | 1953 |
| *Il Bidone* | Federico Fellini | Italy | 1955 |
| *Journal d'un curé de campagne* | Robert Bresson | France | 1951 |
| *Un condamné à mort s'est échappé* | Robert Bresson | France | 1956 |
| *Mouchette* | Robert Bresson | France | 1966 |
| *Le Feu follet* | Louis Malle | France | 1963 |
| *Hunger* | Henning Carlsen | Scandinavian co-pr. | 1966 |
| *The Round-up* | Miklos Jancso | Hungary | 1965 |

Antonioni's *L'Eclisse* was scheduled but no available copy could be found in Europe

## Subjective film

*Silent*

| | | | |
|---|---|---|---|
| *Cabiria* | Giovanni Pastrone | Italy | 1914 |
| *Intolerance* | D. W. Griffith | U.S.A. | 1916 |
| *Strike* | S. M. Eisenstein | U.S.S.R. | 1924 |
| *The Battleship Potemkin* | S. M. Eisenstein | U.S.S.R. | 1925 |
| *October* | S. M. Eisenstein | U.S.S.R. | 1928 |
| *Old and New* | S. M. Eisenstein | U.S.S.R. | 1929 |
| *Earth* | Alexander Dovzhenko | U.S.S.R. | 1930 |
| *Sunrise* | F. W. Murnau | U.S.A. | 1927 |
| *People on Sunday* | Robert Siodmak | Germany | 1929 |
| *I Was Born, But . . .* | Yasujiro Ozu | Japan | 1932 |

*Sound*

| | | | |
|---|---|---|---|
| *Un Chien andalou* (synchronized) | Luis Buñuel | France | 1928 |
| *L'Age d'or* | Luis Buñuel | France | 1930 |
| *Terre sans pain* (*Land without Bread*) | Luis Buñuel | Spain | 1932 |
| *Zéro de conduite* | Jean Vigo | France | 1933 |
| *L'Atalante* | Jean Vigo | France | 1934 |
| *Citizen Kane* | Orson Welles | U.S.A. | 1941 |
| *Rashomon* | Akira Kurosawa | Japan | 1950 |
| *Ugetsu Monogatari* | Kenji Mizoguchi | Japan | 1953 |
| *Persona* | Ingmar Bergman | Sweden | 1966 |
| *Passenger* | Andrzej Munk | Poland | 1963 |
| *Wild Strawberries* | Ingmar Bergman | Sweden | 1957 |
| *Le Petit Soldat* | Jean-Luc Godard | France | 1960 |
| *Alphaville* | Jean-Luc Godard | France | 1965 |
| *Otto e mezzo* (*8½*) | Federico Fellini | Italy | 1963 |
| *Hiroshima mon amour* | Alain Resnais | France | 1959 |
| *L'Année dernière à Marienbad* | Alain Resnais | France | 1961 |
| *Muriel* | Alain Resnais | France | 1963 |
| *La Guerre est finie* | Alain Resnais | France | 1966 |
| *This Sporting Life* | Lindsay Anderson | Britain | 1963 |
| *Barrier* | Jerzy Skolimovski | Poland | 1966 |
| *Herostratus* | Don Levy | Britain | 1968 |

## Factual and Short films

| | | | |
|---|---|---|---|
| *Ninety Degrees South* (synchronized) | Herbert Ponting (1912) | Britain | 1934 |
| *Paris 1900* | Nicole Védrès | France | 1947 |
| *Nanook of the North* | Robert Flaherty | U.S.A. | 1922 |
| *Moana* | Robert Flaherty | U.S.A. | 1926 |
| *Man with a Movie Camera* | Dziga Vertov | U.S.S.R. | 1928 |

CONTINENTAL DOCUMENTARIES

| | | | |
|---|---|---|---|
| *Rain* | Joris Ivens | Holland | 1929 |
| *Easter Island* | Storck-Ferno | Belgium | 1934 |
| *Romance sentimentale* | Alexandrov | France | 1934 |
| *L'Hippocampe* | Jean Painlevé | France | 1934 |
| *New Earth* | Joris Ivens | Holland | 1934 |
| *Les Maisons de la misère* | Henri Storck | Belgium | 1937 |

BRITISH DOCUMENTARIES

| | | | |
|---|---|---|---|
| *Pett and Pott* | Alberto Cavalcanti | Britain | 1934 |
| *Song of Ceylon* | Basil Wright | Britain | 1935 |
| *And So to Work* | Richard Massingham | Britain | 1936 |

GERMAN DOCUMENTARIES

| | | | |
|---|---|---|---|
| *Berlin, Symphony of a Great City* | Walther Ruttmann | Germany | 1927 |
| *The Triumph of the Will* | Leni Riefenstahl | Germany | 1935 |
| *1936 Olympic Games* | Leni Riefenstahl | Germany | 1937 |

SHORT FILMS BY ALAIN RESNAIS

| | | | |
|---|---|---|---|
| *Van Gogh* | Alain Resnais | France | 1948 |
| *Guernica* | Alain Resnais | France | 1952 |
| *Nuit et brouillard* | Alain Resnais | France | 1956 |
| *Toute la mémoire du monde* | Alain Resnais | France | 1956 |

| | | | |
|---|---|---|---|
| *Native Land* | Strand-Hurwitz | U.S.A. | 1942 |
| *Four Days of Naples* | Nanni Loy | Italy | 1962 |
| *Loin du Vietnam* | Godard/Ivens/Klein/ | | |
| | Lelouch/Resnais/Varda | France | 1967 |
| *The Italian Conquest of Abyssinia* } | Two films dove-tailed | U.S.S.R. | 1938 |
| *The Path of the Heroes* } | | Italy | 1938 |
| *The War Game* | Peter Watkins | Britain | 1965 |
| *Warrendale* | Allan King | Canada | 1966 |

| | | | |
|---|---|---|---|
| *Time Is* | Don Levy | Britain | 1965 |
| *Opus* | Don Levy | Britain | 1967 |
| *Five Shorts* | Don Levy | Britain | 1968 |
| *La Jetée* | Chris Marker | France | 1963 |

The aim of these programmes was to show the work of a few outstanding artists. Certain classic examples, key films, are not always available for programme building. The films listed were those that were screened, except *L'Eclisse*.

# Bibliography of some relevant recent books

BADDELEY, W. HUGH, *Documentary Film Production*, Focal Press, London, 1969.

BAZIN, ANDRÉ (tr. Hugh Gray), *What is Cinema?* University of California Press, Berkeley, 1967.

BOBKER, LEE R., *Elements of Film*, Harcourt, Brace and World Inc., New York, 1969.

BOUSSINOT, ROGER, *L'Encyclopédie du cinéma*, Bordas, Paris, 1967.

BRYNE-DANIEL, J., *Grafilm*, Studio Vista, London, 1970.

COLPI, HENRI, *Défense et illustration de la musique dans le film*, S.E.R.D.O.C., Lyon, 1963.

———, *Enciclopedia dello Spettacolo*, Unione Editoriale, Rome, 1966.

ESNAULT, PHILIPPE, *Chronologie du cinéma mondiale*, Les Grands Films Classiques, Paris, 1963.

FIELDING, RAYMOND, *Special Effects and Cinematography*, Focal Press, London, 1965.

FIELDING, RAYMOND (ed.), *A Technological History of Motion Pictures and Television* (An anthology from contributions to the Journal of S.M.P.T.E.), University of California Press, California, 1967.

———, *Filmlexicon degli Autore e delle Opere*, Bianco e Nero, Rome, 1967.

GEDULD, HARRY M. (ed.), *Filmmakers on Film Making*, Indiana University Press, Bloomington, 1967.

GUBACK, THOMAS H., *The International Film Industry*, Indiana University Press, Bloomington, 1969.

HALAS, JOHN, AND ROGER MANVELL, *The Technique of Film Animation*, Focal Press, London 1968.

HOUSTON, PENELOPE, *The Contemporary Cinema*, Penguin Books, London, 1963.

HUACO, GEORGE A., *The Sociology of Film Art*, Basic Books Inc., New York, 1965.

JACOBS, LEWIS (ed.), *The Emergence of Film Art*, Hopkinson and Blake, New York, 1969.

JOBES, GERTRUDE, *Motion Picture Empire*, Archon Press, Hamden, Connecticut, 1966.

LAWSON, JOHN HOWARD, *Film: the Creative Process*, Hill and Wang, New York, 1963; Transatlantic Book Service, London.

MACGOWAN, KENNETH, *Behind the Screen*, Delacorte Press, New York, 1965.

MANVELL, ROGER, AND JOHN HUNTLEY, *The Technique of Film Music*, Focal Press, London, 1957.

MITRY, JEAN, *Dictionnaire du cinéma*, Larousse, Paris, 1963.

———, *Esthétique et Psychologie du cinéma*, vols. i and ii, Éditions Universitaires, Paris, 1965.

———, *Histoire du cinéma*, Éditions Universitaires, Paris, 1967.

MONTAGU, IVOR, *Film World*, Penguin Books, London, 1963.

NISBETT, A., *The Sound Studio*, Focal Press, London, 1963.

POLIERI, JACQUES, ' "Aujourd' hui" art et architecture', *Scénographie nouvelle*, numéro 42–3, Paris, 1963.

QUIGLEY JR., MARTIN, *New Screen Techniques*, Quigley Publications Co., New York, 1953.

REISZ, KAREL, and GAVIN MILLAR, *The Technique of Film Editing*, second enlarged edition, Focal Press, London, 1968.

ROBINSON, W. R. (ed.), *Man and the Movies*, Louisiana State University Press, Baton Rouge, 1967.

SADOUL, GEORGES, *Histoire du cinéma mondiale*, Flammarion, Paris, 1962.

———, *Dictionnaire des films*, Éditions du Seuil (Collection Microcosme), Paris, 1965.

———, *Dictionnaire des cinéastes*, Éditions du Seuil (Collection Microcosme), Paris, 1965.

SARRIS, ANDREW, *Interviews with Film Directors*, The Bobbs-Merrill Co. Inc., New York, 1967.

SOUTO, H. MARIO RAIMONDO, *The Motion Picture Camera*, Focal Press, London, 1967.

TALBOT, DANIEL (ed.), *Film, an Anthology*, Simon and Schuster, New York, 1959.

VIVIÉ, JEAN, *Historique et développement de la technique cinématographique*, Éditions B.P.I., Paris, 1945.

WHITE, D. M. and R. AVERSON (eds.), *Sight and Sound, and Society*, Beacon Press, Boston, 1968.

# Index

G.P.O. film unit, 67; *Henry V*, 79 (*see also* French films, *Les Enfants du Paradis*); *If*, 138; independent frame, 30 n.; Ministry of Information, the (British), 8, 67, 77; national output 1936, 66; new film-makers, 77; pre-1914, 31; propaganda, 31, 67; 'quota quickies', 31 and n., 67; Second World War, 8; slump, 67; War Office, 8

camera, 13, 76; Akeley, 27; Prizmacolor, 27; early, 14, 16, 30 n.; hand-held, 61, 115; recording machine, 14; selection, emphasis, and timing in, 2, 95 (*see also* editing); sound-proof, 56; Stroheim edited in, 21, 62; triple c.s. linked, 106

cameraman, 17, 18; attitudes to sound, 55; factual films, newsreels, 26, 80; Figueroa, Gabriel, 7 n.; Godard's, 115; Toland, Gregg, 70, 75; Vertov, Dziga, 26, 115 n.

camera work, 1, 2, 14, 63, 80; Antonioni's, 112; close-up, 13, 14, 20, 24, 59, 70; dramatic, 16; Eisenstein's (by Tisse), 24; Fellini's, 98, 113; film-making without a director, 26; Flaherty, 27; fragmentation, 63; fragmentation conviction shot, 109; Griffith's (by Billy Bitzer), 19–21; hand-held, 61; long-shot, 20, 64 n.; mid-shot, 20; musicals shot to pre-recordings, 58; sound complicates shooting, 55; storyboard, 29; Stroheim and Phase Three, 22; three-dimensional, 106

canned play, *see* theatrical picture

cannibalism, 108 and n.

cartoons, 31 n.

censorship (first factor), 6, 24, 59, 65, 117 (*see also* political influences and war); Britain, 59, 73 and n.; Communist countries, 118; Europe, 24; France, 67, 68, 73 and n., 78; Germany, 24, 28, 72; Italy, 15, 72, 74, 80, 82; Japan, 72; U.S.A., 18, 20, 65; U.S.S.R., 22, 24, 66, 73 and n.

Centro Sperimentale di Cinematografia, 74, 81, 118; Renoir, 73

chamber films, 28, 84; *see* German films, theatrical picture

*champs contre-champs*, 70

change-over 1929, crucial eight months, 64; physical conversion, 63–4; silence to sound, 53; survival price, 64; Warner Bros., 8–9, 9 n.

Chrétien, Henri, developed anamorphic lens in periscopes for new tank weapon in 1914–18 War, 106; *see* anamorphic lens, CinemaScope, Phase Three

Ciné-Club Liberté, 72; *see* film societies

ciné-clubs, 33, 121; *see* avant-garde, film societies

cinema, concept of, 1, 3, 21, 24 n., 33, 53, 55, 103, 110, 111, 136–7

CinemaScope, 110; print, 4 n.; *see* aspect ratio

cinema screen, *see* aspect ratio

Cinémathèque française, 114–15

cinéma vérité, 26, 115 n.

Cinerama, 106: *see* aspect ratio

colour photography, 2, 14, 86; with anamorphic lens, 108; early, 14; early two-colour, 26; Flaherty, 27; dramatic, 108; 1. Additive processes, 27, 27 n.; Kinemacolor, 26; Prizmacolor, 27; 2. Subtractive processes, 27 n.; Technicolor, 75

comic films, 15–16, 32–3, 34, 85; *see* Westerns

commerce, commercial, *see* conformists

compilation film, 23

conformists (commerce), 5 and n., 63, 103, 105, 109, 119, 121, 135, 136; brave gamble 1929, 64; needs of commerce, 8; *Règle du jeu, La*, 72; and Stroheim, 62; television threat to, 108; under-nourished French, 16; *see* Hollywood, *movie*, United Artists

Continental Films S.A., Paris, *see* Goebbels (78)

conviction shot, 109

co-operative production, *Marseillaise, La*, *Monsieur Vincent*, 138; Underground, 117

'creative interpretation of reality, the', 25–6; *see* documentary film

critic, film (reviewer/theoretician), 5, 6; blinkers, 7; Chaplin, 32; criticism, 7, 137; film festivals, 119; fragmentation, 109; *If*, 138; Mayer, Carl, 7; montage, 62; Phase Three, 110; trained, 137; wider screen, 109, Zavattini, Cesare, 7

Crown Film Unit, 67; *see* Ministry of Information, National Film Boards

cylindrical phonograph records, early sound, 14; *see* synchronization

Czech films, 117, 118

Danes, the, 84, 143

deep focus, 2, 8, 9 and n., 13, 62, 66, 105, 107 (*see* emulsion, lighting, orthochromatic, stopping down); Chrétien's system, 107; early panchromatic, 70; Lumière's, 109; Renoir's need for, 70; Stroheim's use of, 22, 62; Toland, 70, 75; *see* cameraman

Depression, the Great (1929), 64, 66

design, 3; German, 29, 30, 57; models, 61; trick shots, 57, 61; *see* acting, dwarfs

designers, 6, 30; *see* storyboard

disc, sound on, 9 n., 14; *see* Warner Brothers

direct cinema (American), 115 n.; *see* cinéma vérité

director, film, 3; American, 6; French (director as 'interpreter', *see* réalisateur), 3, 5; Griffith, 16; 1929, 63; Phase Three, again dominant, 110; sound-track mediocrity, 9 n., 55; subordination to designers, 29–30; *see* metteur-en-scène, réalisateur

director, assistant, 65; Griffith's, 21; Stroheim, 21

director, dialogue, 55

distortion, of films, 23, 117; import of scripts reversed, 28; variations in third negatives, 20 n.; *see* mutilation of films

distributor, film, 15, 103, 119, 135–6, 149; Chaplin, 32; Ciné-Club Liberté, 72; closed shops, 117; film festivals, 119; Film Society, The, 33; fixed premises, 15; 1946–50, 86; Pathé and U.S.A., 15; Star Film Co., 15; stop-gaps 1929, 63; Underground, 117; United Artists, 19 n., 117; video-cassettes, 145–6; wider screen v television, 86; *see* mutilation of films

documentary film, Eisenstein, 25; factual film, 25–6, 30; with colour, 108; 'the creative interpretation of reality', 25; Vertov and Flaherty, 115 n.

double feature programme, 31 n., 33–4

drawing board, 3, 29

dubbing, 4 and n., 57, 80–1; *see* acting, distortion, remake, synchronization, synthesis

Eady Fund, 142 and n.; *see* British, Hollywood, and Swedish films

Ealing Studios, 77

ear, human, 56

editing, film, 1 n., 2–4, 21, 24; American, 3; close-up, 59; early sound (single

obsolete, 109; *plan-séquence*, antithesis, 110; Renoir and, 69
French films, 66, 72; ciné-clubs, 33–4; cinéma vérité, 115n.; Clair, René, 34, 61, 68; composers, 83; cosmopolitan, 34; cultural missions, 73; decline, 1917, 16; Dreyer, *Joan of Arc*, London, 58; *Enfants du Paradis, Les*, 79 (*see Henry V*, British films); *film d'art, le*, 14, 16; film-makers, 69; German musical films, Paris, 58; late Thirties, 69; neo-realism, 77, 84; no French sound system, 58; nouvelle vague, 114–15; Pathé Frères, 15; *Règle du jeu, La*, 72–3, 137 (*see* factors); renaissance, 79; Renoir and French Communist Party, 71; Renoir and Visconti, 71; short, experimental, 114; silent, 33–5; slump, 66; *Sous les Toits de Paris*, 61; and South America, 117; Tobis-Klangfilm and *Kermesse Héroïque, La*, 69; trade unions, 66, 72; under Nazis, 77–9; *see avant-garde*, British films, censorship, film schools, nouvelle vague, political influences, war
Free Cinema (British), 139
Free Tribune of Cinema, The, 33
Friends of the Seventh Art, The (ciné-club), 33
'Front Office', 32

gangster films, 67; *see* Westerns
*Gas Masks*, 23; *see* Eisenstein
General Film Corporation, 1910–19, 16n.; *see* Motion Picture Patents Co.
German films, 66; chamber films, 28, 84 (*see film d'art, le*); design, 28–30, 57, 61, 74; early sound, 57; Expressionism, 6, 7; golden age, 29; 'hot-house', 29; influence of theatre, 30; Kultur-film, 30; Méliès School, 28; music, 57; musicals, 58; 1929–33, 57; opera, silent film, 35; studio expertise, 28, 29, 68; talent to Hollywood, 29; Tobis-Klang-film in Paris, 58; *see* acting, Berlin, censorship, designers, *Gone with the Wind*, Hollywood, political influences, script-writers, war
G.P.O. Film Unit, General Post Office (British), 67; budget, 67; Cavalcanti, Alberto, 67; Grierson, John, 67; *see* Crown Film Unit, Empire Marketing Board

Grand Café, Paris, 1895: Lumière Brothers, exhibition, first public, 8
Great Patriotic War, The, 77; *see* war, political influences

Holland, feature films, 140
Hollywood, and banks, 9n., 29, 31; and *film*, 7, 9n.; and *movie*, 3, 7, 9n.; Alexandrov, Grigori, in, 66; Antonioni in, 98; aspect ratios, 63; Britain in war, 77; Depression, 64, 66; 'down to earth', 29; Eisenstein in, 66; fills vacuums, 30, 64; films, foreign versions, 58; Fox, William, 29; gangster films, 67; Garbo, Greta, 74; German inflation, 29; Germany and last silents, 29, 74–5; great gamble, 64; home markets, 103; immigration, 29, 31, 141; imports talent, 32; location work, 85; McCarthy, Senator, in, 86; methods, 3–4, 19, 57, 64, 103; Metro-Goldwyn-Mayer, 74, 113n.; motor car, impact on, 86; neo-realism, influence on, 84–5; *October*, 25; post-Second World War, 103; psychologists fail, 85; 'quota quickies', Britain, 31; rejection by Europe, 85; re-recording, 1932, 85; sausage machine, 22, 57; Soviet Union, 85; Stroheim in, 22; survival *v* quality, 64; team work, 64; television, impact on, 86; UnAmerican Activities Committee, 86; use of sound, stunt, 35; Welles in, 75–6; Westerns, 4, 32–3, 64–5, 85; world markets, 31, 32, 57, 74, 75, 85, 103; *see* Berlin, British Film Fund, Tobis-Klangfilm
Hungarian Film Institute, 148

illusion, 1, 2, 29; *see* German films
Imperial War Museum, 34n.
improvisation, 3, 62; neo-realists, 81; Godard, 115; Vertov and Flaherty, 115n.
Indian films: *film* and *movie*, 4; melodrama, 67; Satyajit Ray, 121
inflation, German, 24 and n., 28; *see* Berlin, German films, Hollywood
Institut d'hautes Études Cinémato-graphiques (IDHEC), 114, 118; *see* film schools
International Workers' Aid: *Intolerance* into U.S.S.R., 22–3; *see* Berlin
Italian films, 6, 7, 15, 66, 82–3; Antonioni, 111–13; influence on Bresson, 84;

cultural missions from France, 73; ciné-clubs, 44; dubbing, 4 and n., 80; Fellini, 111–13; Hollywood influenced by, 85; location work, 80; neo-realist school, 6 (*see* Huaco, Geo. H.); neo-realism out of liberation, 79–82; neo-realism outside Italy, 83; neo-realism declines, 80, 111; neo-realism key to Phase Three, 81; Stroheim to Renoir to neo-realism, 22; Visconti and Renoir, 71, 74; *see* Centro Sperimentale di Cinematografia, political influences
Japanese films: introduction to west, 120–21; *Seven Samurai, The*, 4
Joinville Studios, 66, 67; Korda and Cavalcanti, 67; American films, 58; Paramount, 66

Kinemacolor, 26; *see* colour
Kino-Eye, 115n.; *see* Vertov, Dziga
Kultur-Film: German factual film, 30; *see* documentary, German films

*language* (French), 20n.
language (English): American derivations, 4n.; British derivations, 4n.
language barrier: accent, 4 and n.; colloquialism, 59; dialect, 4; dialogue, 57; internationality of silent films, 31, 57; translations, 4, 31, 35, 57, 81; language versions, 57, 64; talking pictures, 57
languages: in film study, 148; translation problems, 35
Latin cinema, 15; silent cinema, 16; no sound systems, 58
lavender film stock, *see* positive film
lens, *see* anamorphic (9n.), Chrétien, CinemaScope, iron curtain countries (107), Magnascope, Panavision; *also* projection (107, 108)
lighting; arclight, 13; early sound, 55; daylight, 13; incandescent, 13; mercury vapour, 13; normal room light, 115; *see* anamorphic lens, deep focus, ortho-chromatic, panchromatic, stopping down
Lumière School ('Living Picture'), 14, 27, 28; deep focus, 109; 'weapon of Socialism', 28; *see* Méliès School

Magnascope lens, 105; *see* emulsion, projection

study of, 137; Sweden, 140, 141; U.S.A., 108 n., 109 n.; *see* mutilation of films
television commercials: Eisenstein, 62
television tube, 108, 135; *see* aspect ratio
tempo, 1, 2, 16, 21, 59, 110; Griffith, 21; in camera, 110; in cutting-room, 59
theatre, influence of, 2, 3, 6, 14–15, 16, 61, 63, 109; Griffith, 1913, 16; Reinhardt, Max, 28, 29
theatrical picture (often canned play), 6, 13, 14, 55, 61, 64, 69, 80, 81; Berlin, 24; chamber films, 28; *film d'art, le,* 14; re-recording kills canned play, 58; stop-gap, 63; uninterrupted scene *v* fragmentation, 109; *v* neo-realism, 80, 81
theoreticians, *see* critics
third dimension, 1, 2; 3-D, 106, 108
'third eye', 21, 25
'time' in film, *see* ambiguity in film time
Tobis-Klangfilm (incorporating Tri-Ergon sound system), 57, 58, 68; Sweden, 141
'trade follows the film', 30
trade unions, French: anti-foreigners, 66; Ciné-Club Liberté, 72; *see* co-operatives (108)
Tri-Ergon sound system, *see* Tobis-Klangfilm
'Trust, The': Motion Picture Patents Corpn., 16 n.; rebellion against, 16
Twentieth Century-Fox Film Corpn., 9, 85; CinemaScope, 1952, 107
Two Cities Films, Ltd., 77

UnAmerican Activities Committee, 85–6
Underground films: distribution, 117
United Artists Corpn., 19 n., 117
Universal Pictures Corpn., 56; *see* pre-rererecording

video-cassette (video-player), 145–6, 149
Vieux-Colombier, Théatre du, 33; *see* Jean Tedesco

war (first factor), 6, 53, 103, 106; *see also* censorship, political influences; First World War, effect on: Britain, 31; Europe, 30; France, 15–16, 114; Germany, 6, 28, 72; Italy, 6, 15, 72; Japan, 72; U.S.A., 22, 30; U.S.S.R., 6, 53; Second World War, effect on: Britain, 8, 77, 103; Europe, 85, 103; France, 77–9, 103, 114; Germany, 57, 73, 77, 85, 103; Italy, 6, 73–4, 77, 85, 87, 103;

Japan, 85, 87, 103, 120; U.S.A., 74, 85–6, 103; U.S.S.R., 28, 77, 87, 103; Sweden, 141
Warner Brothers Corpn., 8–9, 9 n.
'weapon of socialism': Lumière School, 28
Western Electric sound system: German Tri-Ergon patents, 57; *see* Berlin, Tobis-Klangfilm
Westerns, 4; in terms of cinema, 33; on location, 32, 85; rival subjects, 67; *Stagecoach,* 64–5; *Ride Lonesome,* 110

# People

Alexandrov, Grigori, 25, 61, 66
Allenby, General, 149 n.
Anderson, Lindsay, 138–9
Andreotti, Guilio, 80
Antonioni, Michelangelo, 3 n., 72, 83, 109, 111–12, 138
Autant-Lara, Claude, 106

Balcon, Sir Michael, 77
Barbaro, Umberto, 15, 79
Barry, Joan, 61 n.
Bazin, André, 109
Bergman, Ingmar, 84, 141
Bernanos, Georges, 84
Bernhardt, Sarah, 14
Bertini, Francesca, 15
Blasetti, Alessandro, 81
Boetticher, Budd, 109
Bresson, Robert, 3, 84, 114
Buñuel, Luis, 7, 34, 67

Cain, James, 74
Canudo, Ricciotto, 33
Canutt, Yakima, 65
Carné, Marcel, 6, 69, 71, 79
Cary, Joyce, 135
Castellani, Renato, 83
Cavalcanti, Alberto, 34, 67
Chabrol, Claude, 114, 115
Chaliapin, Fyodor, 58
Chaplin, Charles, 5, 15, 19 n., 32, 33, 35, 73, 84, 102
Chekhov, Anton, 72
Chrétien, Henri, 106, 107
Christ, Jesus, 19

Churchill, Winston, 59
Clair, René, 34, 35, 58, 61, 68, 69, 73
Cloche, Maurice, 138
Cocteau, Jean, 5, 34, 67
Cooper, Merian C., 107
Coquelin, 14
Corvo, Baron, 76

del Giudice, Filippo, 77
Delluc, Louis, 33, 34
Demy, Jacques, 114
de Rochement, Louis, 85
de Santis, Guiseppe, 73, 82, 83
de Sica, Vittorio, 73, 81, 82, 84, 111
Diaghilev, Serge, 5
Dietrich, Marlene, 31
Donner, Jorn, 141
Dovzhenko, Alexander, 27
Dreyer, Carl, 29 n., 58, 84
Dulac, Germaine, 34
Duse, Eleanora, 14
Duvivier, Julien, 69

Eady, Sir Wilfred, 142 n.
Eisenstein, S. M., 15, 22, 23–6, 28, 61–3, 66, 73, 76, 84, 109, 115; *see also* bifurcation
Emmer, Luciano, 83
Epstein, Jean, 34
Ermolief, 34

Fairbanks, Douglas (sr.), 19 n.
Fellini, Federico, 83, 111, 112
Feyder, Jacques, 68, 69
Fields, W. C., 19
Figueroa, Gabriel, 7 n.
Flaherty, Robert, 27–9, 84, 115 n.
Ford, John, 65
Fox, William, 29
Franju, Georges, 114
Frederick, Pauline, 35

Gance, Abel, 69, 106
Garbo, Greta, 74, 141
Pietro, Germi, 83
Gish, Lilian, 24
Gliese, Rochus, 29
Godard, Jean-Luc, 114–16
Goebbels, Dr., 69, 73, 78
Gorky, Maxim, 71
Grémillon, Jean, 34
Grierson, John, 25, 31, 67

# Films